Perfect Wedding Processionals

About the Series

The Romantic Wedding Rituals series is a collection of definitive guides to symbolic rituals used in wedding and commitment ceremonies.

Other titles in the series
Unity Candle and Sand Ceremony
A Definitive Guide to the Creative Use of Candles and Sand Rituals in Wedding and Commitment Ceremonies

How to Write Vows that Wow!

55 Loving Ways to Remember
A Definitive Guide to Including Those Who Have Passed in Your Wedding Ceremony and Celebration

Forthcoming Titles
Fantastic Wedding Finales
A Definitive Guide to Releases, Tosses, Jumping the Broom, and Other Creative Grand Finales for your Wedding or Commitment Ceremony

Other titles are planned to cover the Rose Ceremony, the use of Pebbles and Stones, Handfasting and the use of Ribbons and Cords, and Wine Rituals.

Disclaimer

Although Jennifer Cram has taken every care in preparing and writing this book, she accepts no liability for any errors, omissions, misuse, or misunderstandings on the part of any person who uses it or the associated website. Reliance on the information and material in this book and the associated website shall be at your sole risk. The author specifically disclaims any implied warranties of fitness for any particular purpose and accepts no responsibility for any damage, injury, or loss occasioned to any person as a result of relying on any material included, omitted, or implied.

Perfect
Wedding Processionals

A Definitive Guide to Making a Grand Entrance
for your Wedding or Commitment Ceremony

Jennifer Cram
Authorized Marriage Celebrant

Romantic Wedding Rituals Series

Perfect Wedding Processionals
A Definitive Guide to Making a Grand Entrance
for your Wedding or Commitment Ceremony
First edition.
©Jennifer Cram 2013. All rights reserved.

Front Cover photograph   Jekert Gwapo
Cover Background photograph   © Jinaiji | Dreamstime.com

ISBN-10: 1489518320
ISBN-13: 978-1489518323

SERIES FOREWORD

Wedding and commitment ceremonies require beautiful words. It is the words of the ceremony, particularly those of the promises that the couple makes, that create their union and emphasize what is important to them. However, it is the visual images that linger in the minds of the guests, provide opportunities for amazing photographs, and create truly memorable moments. What would a wedding ceremony be without the image of the ring being slipped onto the bride's finger? Who at a wedding or commitment ceremony doesn't eagerly anticipate the highpoint of the ceremony – the kiss? These images evoke tender emotions and it is emotions that make ceremonies special.

Great wedding ceremony images add drama to the ceremony. Rituals provide the opportunity tell a story that enriches the sentiments that have been expressed and enhances the promises that have been exchanged. Rituals also provide opportunities to express the warmth of the relationship between the couple, their families and friends, and to demonstrate generosity of spirit in acknowledging that every relationship needs the support of others. It is this combination of imagination and creativity with warmth and generosity of spirit that creates a magical ceremony. Inviting those attending your marriage or commitment ceremony to participate in the ritual in some way provides an opportunity to transform the ceremony from being a performance witnessed by an audience of family and friends to a community experience. Including a ritual is also a very effective way to bridge a language gap where you have guests who are not native speakers of the primary language in which the ceremony is conducted.

Rituals in weddings have become fashionable. What a celebrity does in her wedding becomes the *must-have* for countless brides, encouraged by wedding planners who provide a 'check the box' list. Moreover, couples come to believe that there is an 'authorized' form of the ritual to which they are required to adhere. Nothing could be further from the truth.

A ritual is a symbolic act, a visual expression of an intention. When used in a ritual, a symbol is a means by which we convey, in an intuitive rather than logical way, the transcendent. Therefore, a genuine symbol does what it symbolizes. The exchange of vows and rings, now an integral part of any marriage or commitment ceremony, both symbolize and create the union.

Mindless replication or repetition of any ritual has the potential to strip the words, the performance, and the underlying idea of meaning, and therefore you should avoid them. For maximum impact, any symbolic ritual you include in your ceremony needs to truly reflect your unique and wonderful relationship with each other, and/or with your family members and friends. It needs to be personal. It needs to be something you have made your own otherwise it becomes a meaningless distraction.

Reading about a ritual is not enough. Try it out before you make the final decision to include it in your ceremony. Does it feel comfortable for you? Will those attending your wedding 'get it' or will it make them feel uncomfortable or confused? Or even worse, will the ritual seem totally alien to them or just plain silly?

This is not to say you should never include a ritual that no one in your community has ever seen before, but you should assess the extent to which there is a genuine connection between the ritual, the sentiments expressed elsewhere in your ceremony, and your heritage.

This last is particularly important. Avoid cultural appropriation, taking something from a culture with which you have no connection. Particularly, be a little skeptical about claims made that the ritual has its origins 'long ago and far away'. In many cases invented rituals are given an unnecessary and equally invented history to confer legitimacy, when no such history is needed.

When you have chosen to include a particular ritual in your ceremony, think carefully about what it means for you, how you can make it your own. And rehearse and rehearse. For best effect the ritual should be effortlessly performed.

Ensure that both your photographer and your videographer are fully briefed before the day so they know what to expect and where to position themselves to capture the best visual record of the ritual. You may find it useful to provide them with a written summary of how the ritual will unfold.

On the day take your time. Do not rush through the ritual. You will be rewarded with a special moment and a wonderful photographic record.

Enjoy!

JENNIFER CRAM

CONTENTS

INTRODUCTION

Wedding and commitment ceremonies build emotion throughout the ceremony. The guests (and the groom) eagerly anticipate the entrance of the bride and the music and the way that entrance unfolds, sets the mood for the ceremony. For the bride, this is her 'red carpet moment'.

In same sex ceremonies one or both partners may make their entrance in a traditional processional.

The order of a wedding processional follows a general pattern, that general pattern which may vary from place to place and from religious tradition to religious tradition. Civil and non-denominational ceremonies held outside a place of worship tend to follow the processional order most common in the area.

Over the past 40 years the focus of the wedding industry has moved from the ceremony to the celebratory party afterwards, largely because where the ceremony format and inclusions are mandated there is little scope for increasing wedding industry profit by creating demand for additional items or services. As a result the industry has taken a formulaic approach to the ceremony, particularly the processional.

In the 21st century there is greater acceptance of deviating from customary forms. Couples are free to express their personalities in the way the processional is structured and who participates in it. Achieving your vision for your processional may involve some negotiation if you are marrying in church. If marrying in a non-religious or non-denominational ceremony you may need to be assertive with a wedding planner, venue manager, or members of the bridal party. One or more of these may be intent on ensuring that your processional is indistinguishable from that of every other bride who has ever been married in the area.

The processional is extremely important in setting the tone for the ceremony. Yet decisions about it are often an afterthought, left until the last minute after all other choices about the ceremony content have been made. Where decisions about your processional are completely in the control of the wedding coordinator at the venue it will be impossible to stamp your personality on it.

I urge you to consider all the options and make decisions about your processional very early in your wedding planning. Planning your processional will throw up a variety of issues. These, and the solutions you develop, will clarify the atmosphere you want for your ceremony, the traditions you want to honor, the values you wish to communicate to everyone present, and the unique aspects of your relationship and personalities that will make your wedding extra-special.

This book will guide you through a wide range of ways to start your wedding on a high note. It also provides you with information about practical requirements and the .historic and symbolic background to this ritual.

Enjoy your journey through the options and ideas, and have a great wedding with a fantastically exciting and photogenic beginning!

PART ONE:
THE PROCESSIONAL

WHAT IS THE PROCESSIONAL?

The processional is traditionally the formal start to a wedding ceremony. It is the 'curtain up' moment, the moment when the bride, escorted by her father and accompanied by bridesmaids and perhaps one or more flower girls, ring bearers and page boys, enters the church, chapel, or ceremony space and walks down the aisle, through the guests, to take her place next to the groom.

The type of processional you will most frequently see described in the wedding press and included in movies, that is, the processional as the prerogative of the bride, is culturally Christian. In Jewish weddings both bride and groom are escorted down the aisle by their parents, a processional format that is gaining popularity in both secular weddings and weddings in Christian churches as more and more brides choose to have both parents walk them down the aisle.

Some wedding planners, coordinators at some wedding venues, and friends who have been married or have been in a wedding may believe they know the only acceptable way a processional should be done. They may insist you follow their template.

Be assured that there is no such thing as an authorized way to structure your processional. You do not have to rigidly adhere someone else's idea of a proper processional if your style or the values you wish to express would be better served by deviating from the local norm.

The formal walk down the aisle has its roots in the journey of the bride to the groom's home. In Roman times, the ten witnesses required for a Roman marriage accompanied the bride as she made the journey to the groom's family home for the formalization of the marriage. These witnesses have morphed into bridesmaids.

When marriages started to be solemnized at a place of worship the bride and groom, accompanied by their attendants and family members, walked in formal procession to the place where the marriage was to take place. In parts of Europe the tradition of walking to church survives to this day. It is most likely to be observed in local neighborhoods and smaller villages.

During the Middle Ages marriages had to be solemnized in public, so the ceremony took place at the church door. The clergy, bride, groom, their attendants, and their families, then entered the church for a mass, processing down the aisle. As they walked they would chant one of the 15 psalms designated *songs of ascents*.

Later, marriage ceremonies moved inside the church and the processional changed to the model we accept today. The groom enters first, either down the aisle or from a side door, and waits for the bride to make her entrance through the main door and walk down the aisle to stand by his side.

Move into the 20th century, and the customs of the catwalk and beauty pageants move into church, influencing the processional. Each member of the bride's processional now has her own red carpet moment during which she is the centre of attention.

Certain environments, such as a church, synagogue, or indoor ceremony space, call for a formal processional, to the greater or lesser degree following the traditional model. Others, such as outdoor areas or restaurants, may suggest a non-traditional approach. A processional does not have to proceed in a straight line. You can wander down a winding path, walk down a curved staircase, or weave your way through restaurant tables. Where the ceremony is taking place in a small domestic space that does not lend itself to a lengthy formal processional, you may just walk down the staircase, step onto the porch, or walk through a door.

Whatever form it takes, the processional serves a practical purpose – it signals the start of the ceremony in a way guaranteed to grab everyone's attention and allows the bridal party to move into position at the altar in an orderly fashion.

It also serves an emotional purpose and which can be enhanced by including those you love to ensure you have the utmost emotional support as you glide down the aisle. Done well, your processional can be a beautiful and symbolic expression of the joining of two families that your marriage will bring about. It will also allow each of the participants to be acknowledged and individually honored. There is no better justification for including in your processional not only the bride and her attendants, but also the groom, his attendants and other people important to you.

Do not let 'tradition', custom, the general order common in your community, or the processional configuration your particular wedding venue expects you to follow deter you having a processional that matches your vision, nor from including grandparents, step-parents, children from a previous marriage or marriages, babies, or pets.

The way the bride enters is a 'tradition' that has been tweaked, and tweaked, and tweaked again. This should give you the confidence to know that as long as the processional reflects who you are as a couple, both of you are happy with the arrangements, and everyone involved is well-rehearsed so the procession flows smoothly, your processional will not only be fine, but you'll surprise and delight your guests and have fantastic photographs as a memento.

IT 'HAS ALWAYS BEEN DONE THIS WAY'

T he word you will hear more often than any other when you are planning your wedding is *tradition*. The big dirty secret of the wedding industry is that what is repeatedly served up as 'tradition' – the 'way it has always been done' – is largely manufactured, generally expensive, and invariably used to cajole or intimidate brides into focusing on the purchased wedding. This can be cumulative. If something is done often enough by enough brides it becomes easy to claim that it is a tradition legitimized by historical precedent.

Traditions are customs and practices perpetuated because they ground us in our past. It is worth noting that, in Ancient Rome *traditio*, the Latin root of our word *tradition*, meant not only to hand on, but also to hand over. By adapting a tradition in line with your own values you can make it contemporary and meaningful. But you should not be deterred from discarding a tradition that has acquired a negative meaning, or merely has no meaning for you.

Most of the symbols and practices associated with weddings represent practices that were designed to assure fertility or to protect the bride or the couple. Some have roots in a view of the bride as a chattel, now regarded to be totally inappropriate. Those who insist that you must adhere to a certain order in your processional because it is 'traditional' would probably baulk at including the word obey in the bride's vows. Those who insist on an aisle runner, would most likely reject the notion that the bride's feet must be kept from touching the ground lest the evil spirits lurking there rise up harm her.

In the context of your wedding, a tradition that is not meaningful, or cannot be adapted to make it meaningful, has no place. When it comes to the processional, tradition is tradition, not law, and *non-traditional* is not a synonym for *irreligious* or *just plain wrong.* There are no wedding police. If you are being urged to include something on the grounds of tradition, but it won't stand up to close examination, appears faux or silly, will be expensive, or won't actually add meaning to the day, you can pass without a twinge of guilt.

The wedding as we know it is constantly evolving. Professional wedding services are only about a century old. Personalized weddings started to emerge about 40 years ago. The list of what brides are told is required to have a 'proper' wedding has grown and grown. Over the past century or so new 'tradition' after new 'tradition' has been invented and added to the 'proper' wedding, but rarely, if ever, is an earlier tradition eliminated. What used to be optional is now marketed as a must have/must do.

The good news is that there is not a great deal the wedding industry can do to up sell the processional. The bridal bouquet is an early 20th century addition.. Throughout the 19th century and into the early 20th century brides generally carried a bible or prayer book. The flower girl's basket and ring pillow, now available commercially, can just as easily be a DIY project. Indeed the aisle runner (the cloth one as opposed to a carpet) and "Here comes the bride" banners are the sole recent additions to the shopping list, ironically both harking back to the past.

Floor coverings had a practical purpose as well as a superstitious one. When churches had bare wooden floors they kept the bride's dress clean. Modern cleaning practices and carpet runners have made the cloth aisle runner redundant indoors. An aisle runner can be positively dangerous if laid down on a hard floor without being well taped down, and on grass can be quite difficult to walk on because it will move, wrinkle, or be punctured by high heels. Banners were originally standards, cloth versions of a family crest carried in front of important individuals.

Before reacting or becoming upset when family members are insistent that you follow certain 'traditions' take some time to sit down one-on-one with your mother, grandmothers, and, if possible, great-grandmothers. Ask them to show you their wedding photographs and mementos, and encourage them to tell you about their weddings, in detail. Listen carefully for their take on tradition and what they included and the adaptations they made. The simplicity of their weddings may surprise you. It will soon become clear that much of what we are now sold as tradition is relatively new and definitely consumer-oriented, but you will also come to understand what traditions are important to these special women, and why.

Another word used to control brides is *etiquette*. Etiquette comprises behavioral guidelines designed to ensure that that you do your best to be gracious and to ensure that no one is hurt by the way they are treated at your wedding. Etiquette is about taking the feel;ings of your family and your guests into account, however, when it comes to a wedding, much, if not most of what you are told is wedding etiquette that must be followed to the letter, has just been made up.

When the wedding industry tells you something is correct etiquette, the underlying motivation is usually commercial advantage. When your friends and family tell you something is correct etiquette, however, they are more like to be motivated by a lack of confidence and concerns about being judged.

No one will admit to these personal motivations. Instead, they will express concern that if you don't comply people will be offended. Being offended is not necessarily the same as feeling hurt. Offended can just mean that you did not make the choices they would have made. Being hurt means that the person feels that you do not value them.

With love and careful planning it is possible to be true to your vision of your processional and also ensure that everyone present at your wedding feels welcome and valued. Something as simple as making sure you smile and acknowledge your guests as you walk down the aisle will go a long way. But never underestimate the importance of verbal acknowledgement during the ceremony, and of making sure you spend one-on-one time with each of your guests during your reception.

WALK, DANCE, OR ?

Remember the wedding party that danced their way down the aisle (the JK Wedding Entrance that went viral on YouTube)? At the time it was original, but the video has since been seen by millions of people. It was also imitated in a spoof on the wedding of Prince William and Kate Middleton advertising a British telco. As a result it is almost as familiar as a traditional processional. Nonetheless the video is worth watching again because it is a great example of how an original approach to the processional and working with the music to create original moves can maximize you opportunity to design a processional that sets the tone for your wedding, creates the atmosphere for the ceremony and, by extension, for the celebrations to follow, and makes a personal statement. Your processional can display your sense of fun, or it can be a formal reflection of the solemnity of the occasion. Either way, whether consciously or not, your processional makes a statement about your values.

The basics – how to walk down the aisle

I tell my bridal parties that for best effect they should stroll down the aisle in a purposeful though relaxed manner.

At all costs avoid the 'hesitation' step (sometimes called the 'step-togethers') – where you pause between steps with the feet together. It looks ungainly, and because it is unnatural, you will probably wobble, particularly when wearing high heels. You may even overbalance. Not a good look

On the other hand, you definitely do not want to march down the aisle in a military manner. There is a reason why popular military marches rarely make it onto the wedding playlist. Quick marching to a tune more associated with military parades does little to encourage smiling your way down the aisle.

.

MIXING IT UP

Traditionally the bridal party is divided along gender lines, with the bride attended by her sister(s) and/or close female friends, and the groom by close male friends.

While this may be visually attractive because the picture the bridal party presents when standing at the altar is symmetrical, it is not entirely historically accurate. In the Middle Ages the bride stood next to the groom, as she does today, but it was the best man who stood on the other side of bride in order to protect her, ensuring that the wedding went ahead without a hitch.

The groom may have a particularly close relationship with a very supportive sister, or the bride may be close to her brother, and having a best friend of the opposite gender is not uncommon. Hence, it is not unusual for bridal parties to include a best woman[1], man of honor, or even best dog.

Visual symmetry can be maintained by dressing all of the attendants, regardless of gender, in a similar fashion. A simple

---

[1] Rather than using this or similar awkward terminology, it makes sense to use the standard terminology. A best man can support either bride or groom, as can a maid/matron of honor.

solution is to focus on color. If the groomsmen are wearing black suits, a maid of honor supporting the groom would wear a black dress. A best man supporting the bride might wear white pants and shirt with a jacket that is the same color as the bridesmaids dresses.

I have had one bride's guy (the term used in that particular wedding) who insisted he wanted to carry a bouquet, but usually a male standing up with the bride would have a boutonniere to match the bridesmaids bouquets, and a woman standing up with the groom would have a corsage matching the groomsmen's boutonnieres.

SAME SEX CEREMONIES

S ame sex couples are faced with the same decisions about how to structure the processional as those that apply to any other wedding.

You need to decide who will be involved and in what order, and to choose appropriate musical accompaniment. But the one thing you shouldn't do and don't need to do is ape a heterosexual wedding.

Same sex commitment and wedding ceremonies are at the cutting edge in developing creative solutions to adapting gender role stereotyped traditions to up-to-the-minute practices in tune with a more contemporary approach to gender and roles, and brides and grooms are following on.

As you read on bear that in mind and make choices that reflect your wonderful, loving, equal relationship

SEATING OF THE MOTHERS

I n a very formal wedding the mother of the groom and the mother of the bride are the last to take their seats. Formal seating of the mothers takes various forms and many wedding guides suggest that this is part of the processional, possibly music is played while the mothers are escorted down the aisle, and, in a well-managed wedding the entrance of the bridal party follows without a pause between the two events.

There are good reasons to schedule the seating of the mothers as a separate ritual that takes places immediately before the formal start to the wedding, the processional.

- Choosing an appropriate piece of music for the seating of the mothers (and of other honored guests if you wish) creates a change of mood from the more contemplative tone of the prelude music that has been played during the arrival of the guests, and thereby signals the imminent commencement of the ceremony.
- The music you choose can be a graceful way to pay tribute to both mothers, for example *Blest be the Tie that Binds* by Nageli
- Treating the seating of the, mothers as a separate ritual facilitates the first part of a unity candle ritual – the lighting of the side candles by the mothers.

Where you have decided to have the groom and his attendants walk down the aisle in a formal groom's processional, the seating of the mothers will signal the imminent start of two consecutive processionals.

However, for a lovely statement of affection and respect, the groom's processional can be integrated with the seating of the mothers.

WALKING WITH YOU ISN'T GIVING YOU AWAY

For reasons that I've never understood, walking the bride down the aisle seems to be regarded to be an integral part of giving her away. Many brides are uncomfortable with a custom that harks back to times when a woman was her father's property until he handed her over to the groom and she thus became her husband's property. As a result they may deny their fathers the pleasure of displaying his pride and showing his support for the marriage by participating in the processional.

Differentiating between walking down the aisle and being 'given away', widens the possibilities of who might escort the bride. While it is not appropriate for a child to give you away, your child being dependent on you for everything, refocusing this part of the ceremony on both families includes everyone, regardless of age, demonstrates that both families approve the marriage and welcome their family member's spouse, and allows you total freedom of choice of escort.

BRIDAL PARTY ROLES AND RESPONSIBILITIES

Each member of the bridal party has a specific role and specific responsibilities, and these are reflected in the order in which they walk down the aisle and the order in which they stand during the ceremony.

The Bride's escort

Traditionally the bride's father, or her father and mother. However the bride can be escorted by anyone she chooses. She can also choose to walk in alone.

Maid of Honor/Matron of Honor (MOH)

Traditionally the bride's sister or best friend. The MOH is the chief bridesmaid and acts as the bride's witness. During the ceremony she holds the bride's bouquet, checks and helps with the bride's veil, makes sure her train is fluffed and attractively arranged, and generally supports the bride. She may also keep custody of the groom's ring until it is called for before the vows.

Bridesmaid

The role of bridesmaid during the ceremony is purely decorative, although where the MOH needs to have her hands free to arrange the bride's train she can hand off her bouquet and the bride's bouquet to the next bridesmaid in line. Bridesmaids may also assist with children in the bridal party, if necessary walking down the aisle holding their hands.

Junior bridesmaid

A junior bridesmaid is a girl who is too young to be an adult bridesmaid but too old to be a flower girl. She is usually dressed in a similar fashion to the bridesmaids. Her role is purely decorative, though, like the bridesmaids, she can assist with children in the bridal party.

Flower Girl

A flower girl should be at least 5 years old as it is difficult to ensure that younger children are able to behave with aplomb on the day. You need to ensure that she is familiar with her dress, having tried it on a number of times, comfortable with wearing a wreath or flowers in her hair (many younger children are not, and this can cause tantrums on the day). Err on the side of caution and ensure that younger flower girls are guided down the aisle by one of the bridesmaids or an older flower girl.

Historically children are included in the bridal party to ensure fertility and good fortune. In modern times their role is to add a sentimental connection with childhood. Invariably they also add energy, playfulness, and moments of light-hearted and unplanned humor. If the venue allows it, the flower girl scatters rose petals or other flowers and herbs in the path of the bride.

Pageboy/Train Bearer

Pageboys walk behind the bride and carry her train. Including pageboys in the processional is a good idea where the bride's train is very long, or the bridal party needs to walk up steps or on garden paths, as the page boys hold the train off the ground to enable the bride to walk without the train snagging or pulling her back. Because carrying a train requires some strength, coordination, and concentration, pageboys should be about 7 to 12 years old.

Ring Bearer

The ring bearer is frequently a small boy, 3 – 5 years of age, though, as with flower girls, this may be too young to be sure of a polished performance. The ring bearer carries the rings on a pillow or in some other form of decorative container.

There is no reason that the ring bearer has to be male. At the wedding of Princess Victoria of Sweden the rings were carried by a young girl, older than the flower girls, but dressed the same as they were.

Best Man

The best man is not merely the groom's friend, comrade, and witness; he also takes care of many of the practical details related to the wedding. He may keep custody of the bride's ring or of both rings until they are called for in the ceremony. Where clergy and other service providers need to be paid on the day, it is the best man who does this (though most wedding service providers now require payment in advance so this aspect of his duties is fast disappearing). The best man also trouble-shoots when there are last minute hitches with transportation or other arrangements.

Groomsman/Usher

Although each has distinct duties, in many places the terms groomsman and usher are used interchangeably. Ushers are not strictly speaking part of the bridal party. Their task is to greet guests and show them to their seats. They may formally seat members of the bride's and groom's families.

Groomsmen, like bridesmaids, have a purely decorative role during the ceremony. They may, however, be called upon to assist the best man if some remedial action needs to be taken to fix a problem with arrangements.

Pets

An emerging trend is for pets (usually dogs) to be part of outdoor wedding and commitment ceremonies including taking part in the processional. One of the human members of the bridal party should be tasked with walking the pet down the aisle.

Reader(s)

In some churches, it is the custom for a church official to lead the processional while carrying a bible. To acknowledge and emphasize the role of readers, they may participate in the processional, carrying the bible or book from which they are to real, or a decorative folder containing the reading.

Musician(s)

The most frequent example of a bridal party or bride being led in by a musician is the bagpiper at a Scottish themed wedding. However, a violinist, guitarist, a chorale group, or even a mariachi band can serve the same purpose, that is, any musician who is able to walk and play an instrument at the same time can provide the music for the processional while participating in it.

Banner bearers

Small children carrying banners or signs announcing the bride are a recent addition to the processional. In earlier times royal persons were preceded by a standard bearer, a person (soldier or civilian) who carried an ensign or standard used as a formal visual symbol of the person and his/her authority. Standards can also represent a military unit. In religious processions a banner bearing religious symbols may be carried.

Candle bearers

Candle bearers carry lighted candles to light the path of the bride. While not a common inclusion in the processional for best effect have them in pairs. Groomsmen can process carrying candles, as can bridesmaids. When bridesmaids carry candles the candles can be inserted into their bouquets or they may carry them separately.

Candle lighters

Where a formal lighting of candles is a custom of the church, this can be carried out before the bridal party enters. Male candle lighters generally dress in similar fashion to the groomsmen. Female candle-lighters coordinate their outfits with those of the bridesmaids, but do not necessarily match. Candle lighters may be adults or children, the only criterion being that they should be tall enough to reach the top most candles in the tallest candelabra. The candle lighters should light any candles on the end of pews as they progress down the aisle, lighting the candles at the front of the ceremony space, last. They do not light the candles set out for a unity candle ritual. After lighting the candles, they take their seats. At the end of the ceremony, the candle lighters wait until the bridal party and the guests have exited, and then snuff out the candles.

Bell ringer

Originating in the old custom of the church bells ringing to call people into church, a young boy, stands at the entrance to the church or ceremony space and rings a bell to announce the arrival of the bride. Some couples now send a small child, usually a boy, down the aisle, ringing a bell and calling out "Here comes the bride" – a perfect role for an irrepressible youngster who can be counted on to put on a bit of a show.

PUPS IN YOUR PROCESSIONAL

More and more couples are choosing to include their dogs in the ceremony in some way. This emerging trend is an example of the way wedding customs and wedding etiquette is evolving. Just as the specific role and specific responsibilities of each two-legged member of the bridal party is reflected in the processional, so too will the role of your four-legged friend influence where he or she walks in the processional.

There are many roles a dog can play in a wedding:

- Best Dog (or Best Pooch, Pup, or Hound)
- Pooch of Honour (or Pup or Hound of Honour)
- Flower Dog (or Flower Pooch, Pup, or Hound)
- Bridesdog / Groomsdog
- Ring Dog

You need to decide early whether your dog is going to play a formal role in your wedding, or just participate in the processional. But before making a final decision you should assess your dog's personality. A hyper-active or skittish dog may become totally uncontrollable on the day.

And you need to make sure that your dog has intensive training before the day, and a designated minder on the day. Hiring a professional dog minder is a good idea, as that person's sole interest will be the care and control of your pet. The dog minder can ensure the dog is newly shampooed and beautifully groomed, kept calm and cool until brought to the venue just in time to join in the processional. The minder will also ensure the dog has had a timely potty break, and has been given food and water.

If your dog is going to be walked down the aisle, use a lead, and choose a person of appropriate size and strength to hold it. Large dog and small flower girl are not a good mix.

If your dog is tiny, one of your bridal party can carry him or her. Allowing your dog to participate unleashed, relying on verbal commands is not a good idea, if for no other reason that animals are highly sensitive to atmosphere and the heightened anticipation, and possibly anxiety, of the humans that surround the dog, may be unsettling.

STRUCTURING THE PROCESSIONAL

How your processional is structured may differ depending on local customs or cultural practices. The processional always includes the bride, but who escorts her, whether she is on the right or the left of that person, who precedes her and who follows her and in what order, is not universal. The structure of the processional is custom and tradition, not law.

It is well to keep in mind that the practical purpose of the processional is to move the main participants into place so that the ceremony can take place. Should you wish to diverge from local custom, there is no reason why you should not.

Begin the processional with the end in mind. Everyone should know exactly where they will stand during the ceremony and be aware that the processional does not end until everyone is in place. Every other aspect of the processional is what you make it.

The Liturgical Processional

If you are having a formal wedding in church you may be offered a liturgical processional. This type of processional include a crucifer (a person dressed in vestments who carries the crucifix), acolytes who carry candles and/or a banner, together with one or more clergy, who are followed by the bridal party.

The Traditional Processional

The liturgical processional is an act of worship. The traditional processional emphasizes the bride and her bridesmaids.[2]

Traditional Christian practice is that the mothers of the bride and groom are seated last, just before the processional begins. The groom and his attendants move to the altar, the mother of the bride stands, giving the signal for the rest of the guests to stand, and the bride's processional commences. The officiant may lead the groom and his attendants to the altar.

In the United States the bride's attendants enter first. In Britain, the older tradition, followed in the US in the 19th century, prevails. The bride enters first, followed by her attendants. In countries that were formerly colonies of Britain, British practice continues to be adhered to. In others, American practice has been adopted.

In a traditional Jewish ceremony the processional is led by the rabbi, followed by the groomsmen and the groom, escorted by both parents. The bridesmaids, MOH, and the bride, escorted by both her parents, follow.

The Parade Processional

Common in earlier times, the parade processional is still a feature of traditional Scottish weddings. It is beautifully adaptable for non-traditional weddings held in outdoor locations. The groom and the guests gather at a designated place to greet the bride. The groom may assist the bride to alight from her vehicle. Then everyone walks in an informal parade to the ceremony site. The groom escorts the bride. Parents, attendants, and guests follow. A bagpiper or other

---

[2] For convenience I have used traditional bridal party designations, however in the 21st century bridal parties are no longer rigidly divided along gender lines. Bridesguys/bridesmen are joining bridesmaids in supporting the bride and groomsgals/groomswomen are standing up with the groom along with groomsmen.

musicians, followed by the celebrant (officiant) may lead the processional.

Who escorts the bride?

In Christian ceremonies, or civil ceremonies based on Christian traditions (the norm in English speaking countries), the bride is escorted by her father. In Jewish ceremonies, and increasingly in both civil ceremonies and Christian ceremonies, she walks down the aisle with both parents. This is also the only logical choice if your parents are a same-sex couple.

Which side?

It is common for brides to be urged that the 'right way to do it' is to follow the 'tradition', that is that the bride takes her father's left arm when walking down the aisle and that, at the altar, she stands on the left side[3] of the groom. Many wedding coordinators enforce this tradition as if it were a rule, without understanding that the practice evolved for a practical, but outdated, purpose. Both men needed to keep their sword arm free to draw their sword if and when they needed to defend the bride. Because most men are right handed the bride needed to be on the left.

In hundreds of weddings I have never had either man need to do that, though having her father's right arm free does make it easy for the groom to shake his hand before he 'hands over' the bride. It is a 'rule' often broken, even by those whose ceremony choices become the wedding tradition of choice of generations of brides and grooms – royalty. When Kate Middleton married Prince William, she

---

[3] More properly the instruction should be to stand *to stand to the left of the groom*. If the bride and groom stand with their backs to the guests, as is expected in church weddings because the congregation, including the bride and groom, are expected to face the altar, the bride will be on the groom's left. If, however, the couple faces their guests, the bride will be on the groom's right.

walked down the aisle on her father's right arm, as did Princess Diana before her and countless other royal and aristocratic brides. Interestingly, the bridal press and 'how to' books about weddings frequently suggest that the 'traditional' and therefore 'correct' side is the right side. So do whatever works for you.

Who participates in the processional?

Who participates in the processional depends on whether it is the bride's processional, an extended processional or an integrated processional. The groom may also have his own processional, making an entrance down the aisle rather than entering from the side.

The core processional is the bride's processional. It includes the bride, all the members of the bride's party (collectively called *attendants*), together with whoever is escorting her.

An extended processional includes the groomsmen, the bridesmaids, family members, together with others who have a role to play in the ceremony. It may also include individuals carrying items to be used in the ceremony.

An integrated processional combines both bride's processional and groom's processionals, generally with the attendants in pairs. The bride and groom enter together.

Bride's processional

The usual participants for the bride's processional include

- The bride
- The bride's escort(s) – traditionally the bride's father, or father and mother, but can be anyone she chooses, or she can choose to walk in alone
- The chief bridesmaid[4] (Maid of Honor/Matron of Honor)

---

[4] The most senior or chief bridesmaid is usually referred to as the Maid of

- Bridesmaid(s)
- Junior bridesmaid(s)
- Flower Girls

Frequent additions to the bride's processional include

- Ring Bearer(s)
- Page Boy(s)/Train Bearer(s) (who walk in behind the bride and manage her train)

Less commonly, one or more of the following may lead the bride's processional

- Officiant (celebrant or clergy)
- Musician(s) (most frequently the bagpiper at a Scottish themed wedding, but can include a violinist, guitarist, even a mariachi band, i.e. any musician who can walk and play an instrument at the same time)
- Banner bearer
- Candle bearers
- Bell ringer(s)

Groom's processional

The usual participants in a formal groom's processional include

- The groom
- The groom's parents
- The best man
- Groomsmen

One or more of the following may lead the groom's processional

---

Honor (if unmarried) or Matron of Honor (if married). For convenience, she will be referred to as MOH throughout this book.

- Officiant (celebrant or clergy)
- Musician(s)
- Banner bearer
- Candle bearer(s)

Extended processional

An extended processional may include

- Candle lighters
- Readers
- Family members
- Individuals carrying items to be used in the ceremony
- Witnesses if not the best man and MOH
- Groomsmen escorting the bridesmaids

Integrated processional

An integrated processional includes all participants in both the bride's processional and the groom's processional.

Parade processional

A parade professional involves everyone present at the wedding, including guests, parents, bridal party, and officiant.

How many attendants?

It is not uncommon for a bride or groom to be you are being pressured to include numerous family members and/or friends in the bridal party. This may make it difficult to keep the number of attendants, and thus the size and length of the processional, in balance with the number of guests. A smaller wedding calls for a smaller bridal party. One way you can keep your bridal party within bounds is to discard the idea that it has to be evenly balanced. Royal weddings demonstrate this time and again – the bride has more attendants than the groom. But there is no reason why the groom cannot be the one who has the larger number of attendants.

Who goes first?

Accepted practice depends on where you live, on the practices of your community. Because there are no legal requirements for your processional you are free to structure it any way you wish. Personal preference or the constraints of a particular venue may lead you to reverse the order that is the norm in your area.

There are two broad traditions to choose between:
- the bride is preceded by all of her attendants (the norm in the United States and increasingly in other parts of the world)
- the bride is followed by all of her attendants (the older tradition still observed in Britain)

But there is also a third option, one that is as practical as it is unusual. The bride enters in the middle of the bride's processional, preceded by some of her attendants and followed by at least one attendant tasked with managing her train and veil.

Order depends on age, height, and status

When following the American practice of the bride's attendants entering before her, it has become very common for the flower girl(s) and/ring bearer(s) to enter first. On one level this is logical as the attendants are usually placed in order of age, height, and status. Junior bridesmaids enter before the adult bridesmaids with the MOH entering just before the bride.

Unfortunately while logical, it is not always a good idea. Children may be overwhelmed by the experience, particularly if they are quite young, and this can lead to unpredictable behavior. In addition, if the flower girl is scattering petals, every other member of the bridal party will walk over them before the bride does.

A better option is to have the flower girl and ring bearer walk in just before the bride, so that the petals are fresh and the children are confident about where they heading as other adults will already be standing in place.

The adults enter in reverse order to the line-up at the altar. The bridesmaid who enters first should, on arrival at the altar or the ceremony space, move to the position farthest away from where the bride and groom will be standing. Those that follow will fill the space between her and the bride, leaving enough room for the MOH to stand next to the bride.

When following the British practice, the adult attendants enter in the order in which they will stand at the altar – the MOH first. Flower girls and pageboys enter immediately after the bride.

How to structure the processional

There are a number of possible configurations:

1. The groom makes a formal entrance before the bride enters. He can be escorted by his parents, by his best man, by his best man and groomsmen or by his best man, his groomsmen and members of his family.

2. The groom and his attendant(s) – best man and groomsmen - stand up at the front waiting for the bride. The bride's attendants – MOH, bridesmaids, flower girls and pageboys - make a formal entrance followed by the bride, either on her own or escorted by her father, father and mother, or other person.

3. The groom and his attendant(s) stand up at the front waiting for the bride. The bride makes a formal entrance followed by her attendants. Flower girls and/or pageboys walk immediately behind the bride.

4. The groom and best man stand at the front waiting for the bride. Bridesmaids and groomsmen, in pairs, make a formal

entrance. They are followed by the flower girl(s), the MOH, and the bride.

5. Bridesmaids and groomsmen, in pairs, make a formal entrance followed by the MOH and best man, with the bride and groom entering last.

6. Bride and groom enter together. Flower girl(s) and pageboy(s)/ ring bearer, then MOH and best man, and then the bridesmaids and groomsmen, in pairs, follow the couple

7. Any of the variations of the bride entering last can be adapted to the bride entering in the middle, with some of her attendants preceding her, and some following.

IDEAS FROM RECENT ROYAL WEDDINGS

Royal weddings have always been the arbiters of good taste, setting the standard for the "right" way to do a wedding. When you examine how recent royal brides have structured their processionals, however, it becomes clear that there is no single approved form of this most romantic of wedding rituals and that practical considerations can suggest a certain order, for example, one or more adult bridesmaids walking directly behind the bride to manage her train.

Crown Princess Mette-Marit of Norway

When Crown Princess Mette-Marit married Crown Prince Haakon of Norway in 2001 the order of the processional was:

- The bride and groom (bride on the groom's left arm)
- Three young girls holding hands (no flowers)
- Adult bridesmaid holding the hands of a small girl and a small boy

Princess Maxima of The Netherlands

When Maxima Zorreguita married Crown Prince Willem-Alexander of the Netherlands in 2002, the order of the processional was:

- Verger carrying the bible
- Minister

- 6 small children, both boys and girls, walking in pairs holding hands
- The bride and groom (bride on the groom's right arm)
- Two adult bridesmaids
- Two more adult bridesmaids

Crown Princess Mary of Denmark

When Crown Princess Mary married Crown Prince Christian of Denmark in 2002, the order of the processional was:

- bride on her father's left arm
- MOH and one adult bridesmaid walking abreast with two small children between them
- Three junior bridesmaids walking abreast
- Another adult bridesmaid.

Crown Princess Victoria of Sweden

When Crown Princess Victoria of Sweden married Daniel Westling in 2010, the order of the processional was:

- Flower girl and pageboy
- Two flower girls
- Two page boys
- Junior bridesmaid carrying the rings on a pillow
- bride on the right arm of her father, King Carl XVI Gustav
- Three adult bridesmaids walking abreast

The groom and his supporter (best man) waited near the top of the aisle, and when the children had passed them, the groom stepped forward, bowed to the King and took his place on the right side of the bride. The King and the best man then walked in front of the bride and groom, leading the way to the altar..

The Duchess of Cambridge

When Kate Middleton married William, Prince of Wales in 2011, the order of the processional was:

- bride on her father's right hand

- bridesmaid holding the hands of two flower girls
- Two flower girls
- Two page boys

She entered Westminster Abbey with her father and sister. The flower girls were standing waiting at one side. The processional paused to allow the Dean of Westminster to greet the bride, and then, led by the Dean's Verger, followed by the Dean, continued down the aisle.

Princess Charlene of Monaco

When Charlene Wittstock married Prince Albert II of Monaco in 2011, the order of the processional was:

- bride on her father's right arm
- Seven girls all about 7 years old, 3 walking abreast followed by the remaining four girls walking in pairs.

Stéphanie, Hereditary Grand Duchess of Luxembourg

When Countess Stéphanie de Lannoy married Hereditary Grand Duke Guillaume of Luxembourg in 2012, the order of the processional was:

- Two page boys, side by side
- Two flower girls, side by side
- Two flower girls, side by side
- bride on her father's right arm
- Two adult bridesmaids

PRACTICAL ISSUES

Regardless of how you structure your processional there are practical things that need to be managed. These include your veil, your train and your bouquet.

Cuing the Processional

The big reveal of the processional is a big part of the excitement of a wedding. To make it work and that everything happens in the correct sequence and that the music and the processional is perfectly coordinated requires planning, coordination, and communication. You cannot rely on just working to the times in a run sheet, as this could result in prematurely cuing the music. Nor can you always rely on visual cues. There may not be clear lines of sight to the organist or musicians.

You will need to nominate someone to be responsible for communicating that the bridal party is ready to make their entrance to the celebrant (officiant) and to the person designated to cue the start of the music. You will also need to arrange for someone to cue the individual members of the bridal party in order to ensure that they start walking down the aisle at appropriate intervals.

Managing your veil

If you plan to walk down the aisle with your over your face you need to plan for when it will be put back, and who will put it back for you. I always suggest that where your mother and father are escorting you, you mother should be the one to put your veil back. If father is walking you down the aisle, your mother could stand and join you when you reach the top of the aisle and put your veil back. This can be a very emotional and loving moment, allowing both your parents to express their love, and, to exchange hugs or kisses with your groom.

Alternatively, your MOH can put your veil back once you are in place. The third option, keeping your veil over your face until the celebrant (officiant) pronounces that you are married, is not part of the processional.

Managing your train

For best effect, your train should flow naturally behind you when you walk down the aisle. You will need someone to spread it out straight behind you before you take your first steps.

Once you are in place beside your groom, your train will need adjusting again. This is usually the responsibility of the MOH. To free up her hands she will need to hand her bouquet to the next bridesmaid.

If your veil is cathedral length it should be thought of as a second train and adjusted at the same time as your train.

Managing your bouquet

When you are feeling stressed or nervous the flowers tend to go north along with the shoulders. To ensure this does not happen, place the hand in which you are holding your bouquet on your belly button. This also facilitates creating a diamond shape between your arm and your body because your elbow will be directly across from your waist.

For an arm bouquet (also called a sheath) cup your hand round the end of the stems and lay the bouquet along your arm, so that your forearm supports it and the flowers cover the outer side of your elbow.

Who holds whose arm?

For the most formal look, the bride's father holds his forearm parallel to the floor and the bride places her hand on the top of his hand. For a slightly less formal look, her father offers his arm and the bride puts her hand in the crook of his elbow.

To facilitate this, her father should move his elbow away from his body, forming an L-shape with his hand held so that his thumb is roughly in line with his belly button. The bride slips her hand between her father's body and his elbow, from the back, so that her palm rests on his arm and her fingers curve round his arm towards the front.

If there is a significant difference in height between the bride and her father, the only comfortable way for her father to support her may be to cup his hand round her elbow, leaving her hands free to hold her bouquet.

If you are walking down the aisle with both parents, slip your arm through the arm of the parent closest to your own height, and have the taller parent cup your elbow.

When escorting bridesmaids down the aisle, groomsmen offer their arm in the same way as that chosen by the bride and her father.

Regardless of how you choose to do it, relax. Your arms don't need to be stiff.

Bride's Guys and Groom's Gals

Where you have chosen to have both male and female attendants and the groom's attendants are going to meet them and escort them down the aisle, a bridesmaid will enter on a groomsman's arm, but a bride's male attendant and a groomsman or a bridesmaid and a groom's female attendant will walk side by side without linking arms.

Managing your walk

Walk normally, but at a slightly slower pace. Think of it as a purposeful stroll down the aisle, putting one foot after the other with no hesitation, no rocking back on your heels, no bringing your feet together between each step. If the music is about the speed of your walking pace, walk to the beat, but otherwise do not try to keep pace with it.

Steps and stairs

If you have to walk up or down steps, hand your bouquet to your escort.. This will free your hand to lift your skirt or hold onto the banister. As you extend your foot, don't transfer your weight onto it until you can feel the hem of your skirt against your ankle. This ensures you won't stand on your skirt.

It is also a good idea to have the front of your gown hemmed slightly shorter. This can make a great difference to how easily and confidently you can walk up or down steps, along gravel paths, or across lawns. The slight difference in length will not be obvious in photographs.

Sun and shade

Outdoor ceremonies face challenges that do not exist when marrying indoors. One important issue is the position of the sun. If the sun is behind the bride, the groom will not be able to see her facial expression as she walks down the aisle towards him, and for the rest of the ceremony the wedding party will have the sun in their eyes. If the sun is behind the wedding party the bride will see only the groom's silhouette as she walks down the aisle, and for the rest of the ceremony the guests will have the sun in their eyes. Any amateur photos will be disappointing.

One aisle or two

Those marrying in a house of worship may have to contend with two aisles. Two aisles present two problems:

- which aisle to choose to walk down, and
- how to ensure that all guests present are able to see the processional regardless of where they are seated, and that the bride is also able to see the groom as she walks down the aisle.

A simple solution is to use one aisle for the processional, and balance this by using the other aisle for the recessional (the formal exit of the bridal party at the end of the ceremony).

Less common, but better alternatives are to use both aisles for the processional in one of number of ways:

- The groom and the best man enter down the right aisle. When they are in place, the bridesmaids and groomsmen process simultaneously, the bridesmaids down the left aisle, the groomsmen down the right aisle. The MOH follows the bridesmaids. The bride and her escort then process down the left aisle. In a Jewish ceremony the bride may walk down the right aisle, the groom down the left as the bride stands to the right under the chuppah.
- The groom and his parents enter down the right aisle. When the groom is in place, the bridesmaids and groomsmen process simultaneously, the bridesmaids down the left aisle, the groomsmen down the right aisle. The best man follows the groomsmen. The MOH follows the bridesmaids. The bride and her escort(s) then process down the left aisle. It is perfectly acceptable for the groom to be escorted by both his parents regardless if the bride follows tradition and is escorted only by her father.
- The bride's processional and the groom's processional process simultaneously down their respective aisles. The bride and groom, walking either alone or escorted, walk down the same

aisle as their attendants, meet at the front and ascend the sanctuary steps together.

- The groom processes down one aisle with his best man. The bridesmaids, escorted by the groomsmen, process down the other aisle. The MOH follows, walking alone. The bride and her escort follow the MOH.

- The groom processes down one aisle followed by his groomsmen in single file. When they are in place, the bride and her escort, followed by her bridesmaids, process down the other aisle.

For clarity, flower girls, page boys, banner bearers and other participants have been omitted in the above examples.

To ensure that all guests will have a good view of the processional, and that the bride will be able to see the groom and the groom see the bride, it is advisable to request your celebrant (officiant) to ask all guests to remain seated. Alternatively, your celebrant could request that the guests seated in the middle remain seated while inviting those seated in the outer sections to stand. Depending on line of sight, the bride's mother and the groom's parent, who will be seated in the middle pews, may also be invited to stand.

Kiss-Hug/Shake-Hug/Transfer

The processional ends when the bride takes her place next to the groom. When she reaches the top of the aisle, her veil is put back (or lifted) to allow her father to kiss her. The steps forward, shakes the her father's hand (or gives him a hug, or both) and then takes over, escorting his bride the last few steps.

REHEARSE, REHEARSE, REHEARSE

I T is impossible to overestimate the role rehearsing the processional plays in ensuring it goes off without a hitch on the big day, particularly if there are children involved. Unfortunately, many celebrants, particularly those who use a standard ceremony or standard liturgy, discourage rehearsals or refuse to attend them, preferring to leave the management of the rehearsal to the wedding coordinator or wedding planner. Years of experience have lead me to an opposite view. Your celebrant is responsible for stage-managing your ceremony on the day, and it is critical that he/she is involved in the processional from beginning to end, that is, from the design stage to the formal rehearsal.

You may also be told that the bride is not needed at the rehearsal. While that may have been the custom in times gone past, it stems from superstition, from a belief that if the bride participates it will alert evil spirits. We know better. Being actively involved in the rehearsal ensures that the bride, along with the rest of the bridal party, will feel confident on the day and therefore be more relaxed and able to enjoy the ceremony.

Don't just assume that the processional will just happen, playing out perfectly without anyone needing to do anything by way of preparation. If you leave processional decisions to the formal rehearsal you will likely end up with a stock-standard same-old, same-old, walk down the aisle. Design your processional in consultation with your celebrant (officiant), and do that earlier rather than later, and then do all of the following:

- Document your processional in detail and include at the beginning of your ceremony script. If marrying in a religious ceremony following a standard liturgy include the detail of your processional with the list of your choices of hymns and readings.

- Visualize your processional. It might help to have a 'practice' run, or 3 or 4 using tokens or models on a table so you have a 3D view overview. I've had couples use the bride's niece's doll collection, coins or chess pieces to work out the line-up and the flow of the processional.

- Have a pre-rehearsal rehearsal with any children who are part of the bridal party. If you can, have photographs or a video of the aisle to show them. This will help familiarize them with where they will as walking as well as how they will walk down the aisle. Ensure that anything they have to carry is available, that whatever they are to wear on their heads is also available, or, if fresh flowers are planned, some reasonable substitute. If flower girls are to scatter petals, provide a generous amount of substitute petals (torn up crepe paper is works well) and encourage them to keep practicing.

- Ensure that everyone arrives at the formal on-site rehearsal on time and remains focused throughout. Defer socializing until afterwards. That is what rehearsal dinners are for.

- Make sure that your formal rehearsal includes more than one walk-through of the processional and that you practice with the music. Where live musicians have been booked for the rehearsal but are not available for the rehearsal, substitute a recorded version of the processional music.

- Do not forget to brief your photographer in detail so he/she can plan how to shoot your processional photographs..

THE PROCESSIONAL - STEP BY STEP

Every processional incorporates a variety of steps, each of which has to be efficiently managed and accomplished at the designated time, within the allocated time, in order to ensure that, as a whole, it goes off without a hitch.

Because your processional involves walking, if well rehearsed your body will remember where and how to walk, freeing up your mind and your heart to make your way down the aisle with confidence and joy.

For convenience, in the following outline of the processional it is assumed that the bride is escorted by her father and is attended by adult bridesmaids, together with junior and child attendants who walk in before her. You will need to make the appropriate changes to suit your particular situation.

Pre-Processional

The arrival of the groom and his attendants

The groom and his attendants arrive well ahead of the bride. The groomsmen may do double duty as ushers, seating the guests before joining the groom at the altar or waiting ready to escort the bridesmaids down the aisle.

The arrival of the bride's attendants

The bride's attendants arrive before she does. They may travel to the ceremony in a different vehicle, arriving before her and awaiting her arrival, or they may arrive together, in which case they alight from the vehicle first.

The arrival of the bride

The photographer stage-manages the bride's exit from her vehicle. The bridesmaids help with her veil and train. Just before the processional begins the MOH checks that the train is in position to flow smoothly behind the bride as she walks down the aisle.

Cuing the transitional music

The nominated person alerts the celebrant (officiant) to cue the transition music

Forming up

Out of sight of the guests, the bridal party lines up in the order they will process.

Veiling of the bride

If the bride chooses to be veiled for the processional, the MOH will ensure that her veil is in place.

Cuing the processional music

The nominated person informs the celebrant (officiant)that the bride is ready. The celebrant or other designated person cues the processional music.

Type 1 Processional: Bride enters last

The attendants

The attendants walk down the aisle at predetermined intervals, in the order planned, taking their appointed places at the altar, to await the entrance of the bride. A delightful touch is if, instead of just walking past the groom, each bridesmaid takes his hand and gives him a kiss on the cheek.

The bride

[The music changes] The bride, escorted by her father, walks down the aisle.

The groom

The groom moves forward to greet the bride and her father.

Kiss-Hug/Shake-Hug/Transfer

The bride's father puts back her veil (if necessary), kisses or hugs the bride, shakes the groom's hand or gives him a hug. He may place his daughter's hand in the groom's hand, or step aside so the groom may offer the bride his arm. The bride's father takes his seat next to the bride's mother.

Bride and Groom

The bride and groom move to their places ready for the commencement of the ceremony. The MOH arranges the bride's train. She may put back the bride's veil. The bride hands her bouquet to the MOH.

Type 2 Processional: Bride enters first

The bride

The bride, escorted by her father, walks down the aisle.

The attendants

The attendants follow the bride down the aisle at predetermined intervals, in the order planned, and take their places.

The groom

The groom moves forward to greet the bride and her father.

Kiss-Hug/Shake-Hug/Transfer

The bride's father kisses or hugs the bride, shakes the groom's hand or gives him a hug. He may place his daughter's hand in the groom's hand, or step aside so the groom may offer the bride his arm. The bride's father takes his seat next to the bride's mother.

Bride and groom

The bride and groom move to their places ready for the commencement of the ceremony. The MOH arranges the bride's train. She may put back the bride's veil. The bride hands her bouquet to the MOH.

Type 3 Processional : Bride in the middle

The attendants who will precede the bride

Those attendants who will precede the bride start down the aisle at predetermined intervals, in the order planned, and take their places.

The bride

The bride, accompanied by her father walks down the aisle.

The attendants

The attendants follow the bride down the aisle at predetermined intervals, in the order planned, and take their places.

The groom

The groom moves forward to greet the bride and her father

Kiss-Hug/Shake-Hug/Transfer

The bride's father kisses or hugs the bride, shakes the groom's hand or gives him a hug. He may place his daughter's hand in the groom's hand, or step aside so the groom may offer the bride his arm. The bride's father takes his seat next to the bride's mother.

Bride and groom

The bride and groom move to their places ready for the commencement of the ceremony. The MOH arranges the bride's train. She may put back the bride's veil. The bride hands her bouquet to the MOH.

PART TWO:
MUSIC FOR THE PROCESSIONAL

CHOOSING MUSIC FOR YOUR PROCESSIONAL

The music you choose for your walk down the aisle should communicate to everyone present your joy. To achieve that it needs to make you feel happy. It should be easy to walk to, maintaining a steady pace without any sudden changes in tempo. And it should be distinctive.

You can ensure your music is distinctive

- through the piece or pieces you choose
- by presenting the music in an unusual way, or
- simply by choosing pieces that incorporate one or more trumpets. There is no better way to grab the attention of your guests than with a fanfare of trumpets!

Many couples avoid classical music because they feel unsure of their capacity to do choose appropriately. Some will they opt for the default choice, the traditional *Bridal Chorus* from the opera Lohengrin by Wagner. Commonly referred to as *Here Comes the bride,* or *The Wedding March,* it is one of the most widely recognized pieces of music in the western world. Written in the middle of the 19th century, it became popular as the music for the bridal processional after King George V of England chose it for his wedding in 1893. At the time it was regarded to be a daringly modern selection. Ironically, it has fallen out of favor, so it may again be regarded to be a daring and unusual choice if not a common choice in your community.

Before you choose your music you need to know …

Your ceremony venue may constrain your choice of music. Before committing yourselves to any particular musical choice you should have a clear understanding of:

- Any constraint your house of worship, if having a religious ceremony, or your venue, if marrying in a non-religious ceremony, may place on your choice of music or how it is played. Some denominations ban secular music. In many churches this includes *Here comes the bride* together with modern secular songs. Interestingly enough, in England and Wales, where a Registrar will attend a licensed venue to conduct a civil marriage ceremony, many Registrars also ban this piece together with the Mendelssohn Wedding March from a Midsummer Night's Dream on the grounds that, though secular, these pieces are associated with church weddings.
- The policy of your church or venue in relation to hiring outside musicians. Some churches only allow use of the in-house organist, and some venues may have in-house musicians or preferred suppliers.
- Which, if any, instrument is available, for example, is there an organ or piano on site.
- What, if any, equipment is available to play recorded music.
- What styles of music will best express your personalities and suit your ceremony.
- Your personal preferences.
- How long it will take for the whole wedding party to walk down the aisle.

Creating a transition to the processional

Convention suggests that contemplative music should be played for 15 minutes before the ceremony, while guests are arriving and being seated. Consider inserting a musical transition from the prelude music to the processional music to create an emotional bridge between the two.

Playing a popular piece, particularly one with heart-opening, inspiring lyrics, creates the perfect bridge between the quiet mood of the prelude music and the joyous, triumphal mood of the processional music, increases the sense of anticipation in the guests, and helps to settle the bride and groom's nerves.

A love theme will send a powerful signal that the ceremony about to commence is primarily an expression of the love between two people. For example, a good choice would be a stirring sung duet such as Andrew Lloyd Webber's *All I ask from you* from *Phantom of the Opera*.

Another appropriate choice, expressing a different sort of message, would be Puccini's *O Mio Babbino Caro* (Oh my beloved father). In this aria a daughter is asking her father's permission to marry. It will raise a smile in those that recognize it.

An unusual choice, but one that can be very meaningful, is the Click Song, a traditional South African song sung at weddings to bring good fortune to the newlyweds.

If your ceremony will be non-traditional, or if you are including non-traditional elements in the ceremony, transition music can also be used to alert your guests to expect the unexpected.

One piece or two?

Whether you use a single piece of music for your processional or choose one for the entrance of the bridal party and a different one for the entrance of the bride, depends on two things

- The order in which the bride and her attendants walk down the aisle
- Personal preference

If the bridal party enters before the bride, choosing to have a change of music for the bride can enhance the processional. This can either be by having the music played more quietly for the entrance of the bridesmaids and increasing the volume for the entrance of the bride. Because the pieces are played back to back, you should make sure that the two pieces you choose don't clash, but also that they are not so similar that anyone who is not familiar with both won't be able to differentiate between them.

If the bride is entering first, the music is for her. There is no reason to have more than one piece. If the groom is having his own processional, it is usual to choose a piece of music specifically for this.

Or a medley?

Modern technology makes it easy to create a medley of music. If you choose to use a medley and the bride is entering after the bridal party it might be a good idea to insert a fanfare or a few bars of *Here Comes the bride* to signal that the bride is about to make her entrance.

Making the old classical staples new

Choosing one of the old familiar classical pieces has the advantage that your guests will 'get it'. You can make even the most familiar pieces fresh and interesting by giving it a little twist. For example, here are some suggestions:

- The Wagner *Bridal Chorus (Here Comes the bride)*.is usually played on the organ or as a recorded orchestral version. Originally a choral piece, it is lovely when sung by a choir, played on a wide variety of solo instruments from violin to flute, played in an unexpected style, for example jazz, blues, or swing, or played by a brass trio or quartet.
- Jeremiah Clarke's *Prince of Denmark's March* (sometimes called *Trumpet Voluntary in D* and sometimes incorrectly attributed to Henry Purcell), is wonderful played by on a solo trumpet or by a brass quartet

- Pachelbel's *Canon in D* (approved by most Catholic Churches) is lovely played on a piano, an oboe, a cello, or a on a violin, either on its own or accompanying the church organ.
- Bach *Jesu Joy of Man's Desiring, Sheep May Safely Graze,* or *Air on the G String* work well as solo cello, oboe, violin or guitar pieces, or when played by a flute and piano combination. *Jesu Joy of Man's Desiring* also works well when played on a trumpet.

For any piece you can ask your organist to change the registrations, and for any musician you can ask them to tweak the tempo or ask them to be creative in their interpretation of the piece.

Traditional Wedding Songs

Another safe choice are wedding songs that have been around long enough to have become regarded to be traditional . These include the Schubert version of *Ave Maria, Can't Help Falling in Love with You* (Elvis Presley) and *All You Need is Love* (The Beatles). Use the original, another artist's version, a live singer, or an instrumental version.

Modern Wedding Songs

Many brides are now making a very personal choice from a contemporary playlist. If you go down this route it is important to

- Listen carefully to the lyrics to make sure they are suitable for a wedding. It is hard at times to differentiate between a love song and a break-up song.
- Put a note in your wedding program explaining the significance of your choice if the song has personal meaning in your relationship.

Affirm your cultural heritage

Acknowledging your heritage when choosing music for your processional can add a very personal touch. Affirming the cultural origins of both families speaks volumes about your values, and gives you a perfect excuse to create a processional medley.

IT'S ALL ABOUT TIMING

How much time your processional will take depends on the length of the aisle and the number of people who will be walking down the aisle.

Apart from running out of music altogether, leaving some participants to complete the walk in silence, nothing is more awkward than having everyone stand in place while the music just plays on, and on, and on.

Before finalizing your music choices you make sure you have the facts:

- how long the aisle is, i.e. how long it will take for someone to walk the length of the aisle and get into position at a ceremonial pace of walking (a nice easy stroll)
- how much space you intend to allow between the individuals in the processional
- whether everyone walks in separately or some people walk in in pairs

A good rule of thumb is to allow a minimum of 5 paces between people for the processional. However, if the aisle is short you may want to leave a greater distance between them.

The only way to calculate how much music you need is to pace it out, time how long it takes for one person to make the full walk and multiply by the number of individuals/pairs in the processional, and allow for the extra time taken up by the spacing.

Example:

You have decided that your bridesmaids will enter first and you will follow, and that the music will change for the entrance of the bride.

The aisle is 50 paces long and there are 6 individuals or pairs/sets of attendants (for example, two flower girls walking together). You have decided that each bridesmaid will walk 10 paces behind the bridesmaid in front of her, so you need to add 5 "spaces" of 10 paces each to the total of 300 paces that, collectively, your bridesmaids will walk.

When you allow for the spacing between the bridemaids', their part of the processional will take as long as it would take for one individual to walk 350 paces. To accommodate that will need a piece of music that is seven times as long as the time it takes for one individual to walk down the aisle[5].

It is highly unlikely that you will be able to precisely match the length of your chosen piece to the amount of time your processional will take, so you should also decide how you are going to ensure that you neither run out of music or have too long a piece. Some options are:

- Choose a piece that is slightly longer than needed, allowing everyone to take their time to settle into position

---

[5] To ascertain the timing, Have each of the bridesmaids walk down the aisle wearing the shoes they will be wearing at the wedding. People walk differently in heels and each will walk at a slightly different pace because the length of their stride will differ. Work on an average!

- Choose a piece that can be tapered off at a signal to the musicians or the person operating the recorded music. For recorded music fade the music out slowly. Live musicians will need to play to the end of the measure
- Allow a few bars of music to play before the entrance of the first attendant starts walking.

If you are going to play one piece of music for both the bridesmaids and the bride, and the bride and the bridesmaids are entering first you will need to add a few more seconds of music between the entrance of the last bridesmaid and the entrance of the bride. The bride would normally not enter until all the bridesmaids are in place, allowing the groom a clear view of her making her way down the aisle towards him.

MUSIC SUGGESTIONS FOR YOUR PROCESSIONAL

Your processional music sets the tone for your wedding ceremony. Together with lighting, it plays a major role in creating the ambience. However, to be effective, it should be chosen carefully and played at an appropriate volume[6]. This list includes many old favorites and some less well-known selections. Consider it a starting point in your search for the perfect music for your perfect processional.

Classical

Bach: Air on the G String from Suite no. 3 in D Major
Bach: Allegro from the Brandenburg Concerto
Bach: Arioso from Cantata no.156
Bach: Largo from Concerto for two violins in D Minor
Bach: March in D Major
Bach: Jesu, Joy of Man's Desiring from Cantata no. 147
Bach: Sheep May Safely Graze from Cantata no. 208
Bach: Wachet Auf (Sleepers, Awake!)

---

[6] Processional music should be played loudly. You want your guests to sit up and take notice. A common problem, particularly with string quartets and recorded music, and particularly with outdoor ceremonies where the bridesmaids need to walk some distance, is that the music is too soft and they cannot hear when it starts.

Beethoven: Ode to Joy from Symphony no. 9

Bliss: Wedding Fanfare

Charpentier: March from Te Deum

Clarke: Trumpet Voluntary (The Prince of Denmark's March)

Clarke: The Duke of Gloster's March

Debussy: Clair de Lune

Delibes: Flower Duet from Lakmé

Franck Panis Angelicus from Messe Solonelle, op. 12

Greene: Voluntary in D

Handel: Air from Water Music Suite

Handel: Arrival of the Queen of Sheba

Handel Hornpipe from Water Music Suite

Handel Largo from Xerxes

Hollins: Trumpet Minuet

Mascagni Intermezzo from Cavalleria Rusticana

Mozart: Ave Verum Corpus

Mozart: Andante from Divertimento No. 1

Mouret: Fanfare for Trumpet

Pachelbel: Canon in D Major

Purcell: Amphitryon

Purcell: Trumpet Tune

Saint-Saens – Third Organ Symphony (4th Movement)

Saint-Saens – Benediction Nuptiale

Telemann: Andante

Verdi March from Aida

Vivaldi "Spring" from Four Seasons

Wagner: Bridal Chorus from Lohengrin ("Here comes the bride") (for a modern reworking of the theme Romantic Wedding March by Miranda Wong or Bridal March by Jonathan Cain)

Widor: Toccato from 5th Symphony for Organ

From the Movies

Butterfly Waltz from *Twilight - Breaking Dawn*

Happily Ever After from *Ever After: A Cinderella Story*

Kissing You from *Romeo and Juliet*
Love Theme from *Cinema Paradiso*
Moon River from *Breakfast at Tiffany's*
Overture from *The Notebook*
Practical Magic from *Practical Magic*
You're the First, the Last, My Everything from *Four Weddings and a Funeral*
Wedding Processional from *The Sound of Music*

Choral Works – Classical Religious

Bach: Jesu, joy of man's desiring
Bach: May God smile on you
Bach: Now thank we all our God
Bairstow: Though I speak with the tongues of men
Batten: O sing joyfully
Carter: Go before us, O Lord
Carter: God be in my head
Crew: Now lies the earth
Franck: Panis angelicus
Gounod: Ave Maria
Grimm: This is the da
Handel: Rejoice!
Ledger: I will lift up mine eyes
Mathias: Let the people praise thee, O God
Mozart: Laudate Dominum
Parshall: A new commandment
Psalm 45 (44)
Psalm 67 (66)
Psalm 128(127)
Rutter: God be in my head
Schubert : Ave Maria
Vaughan Williams: Come My Way, My Truth, My Life
Vivaldi: Gloria in excelsis Deo (from Gloria)
Walton: Set me as a seal
Willan: Rise up, my love, my fair one

Contemporary Wedding Songs/Anthems

Always and Forever - Heatwave

Amazed - Lonestar

Appalachia Waltz - Yo-Yo Ma, Edgar Meyer, Mark O'Connor

At Last - Etta James

Can You Feel the Love Tonight – Elton John

Can't Get You out of My Head –Kylie Minogue

Can't Help Falling in Love – Elvis Presley

Chapel of Love - The Dixie Cups

Chasing Cars by Snow Patrol

Come Away with Me – Nora Jones

Daydream Believer – The Monkees

Endless Love - Lionel Richie & Diana Ross

Falling In Love at A Coffeeshop - Landon Pigg

Forever And Ever, Amen – Randy Travis

From This Moment on - Shania Twain

(The) Greatest Love of All – Whitney Houston

Have I Told You Lately that I Love You – Van Morrison

Hoppipolla - Sigur Ros

I Do [Cherish You] – 98 Degrees

I do, I do, I do - Abba

I Love NYE - Badly Drawn Boy

I Swear - All 4 One

Isn't She Lovely – Stevie Wonder

Just the Way You Are - Billy Joel

L-O-V-E.- Nat King Cole

Let Me Tell You About My Boat - Mark Motherbaugh

Let's Get Married - The Proclaimers

Longing to Belong - Eddie Veder

(The) Look of Love – Dusty Springfield

Love and Marriage – Frank Sinatra

Love in Any Language –Sandi Patty

Love is All Around – Ricki Lee

(A) Lover's Concerto – The Toys

Marry Me - Train

Me and You – Kenny Chesney

(The) Most Beautiful Girl in the World

My Best Friend - Queen

My Guy

No Matter What - Boyzone -

Not A Moment Too Soon

Reign of Love - Coldplay

Rose Of My Heart - Johnny Cash

She - Elvis Costello

Sky Cloud Winter Breeze - Orba Squara

So Happy Together

Sparkplug Minuet - Mark Mothersbaugh

Third Finger, Left Hand

To the Aisle - The Five Satins

Two People Fell In Love

Unchained Melody – The Righteous Brothers

Unforgettable – Nat King Cole

(The) Vow – Jeremy Lubbock

Walking on Sunshine - Katrina and the Waves

Wedding Song (There is Love) – Paul Stookey

What a Wonderful World – Louis Armstrong

When I'm 64 – The Beatles

When You Say Nothing At All - Ronan Keating

You Decorated My Life – Kenny Rogers

You to Me Are Everything - Barry White

PART THREE:
BANNERS AND SIGNS

HERE COMES THE BRIDE

A recent addition to the bride's procession is a small child carrying a sign saying "Here comes the Bride", This is a visual substitute for the bell ringer. But "Here comes the Bride" is not the only possibility.

To create a more personal sign you could:
- Choose a quotation about love you both like
- Create a relationship time line, for example
  1/1/2012 They met
  2/2/2012 First kiss
  7/7/2012 He proposed
  7/7/2012 She said YES
  Today they say I DO
- Instead of a wooden or chalkboard sign, use a fabric banner hung from a dowel finished with a small finial on each end carried by two children. You can use fabric paint, machine embroidery or appliqué to create the message. If you have a family member who sews or quilts, design your sign early and ask them to make it for you as their gift to you.

PART FOUR:
REACH BACK INTO HISTORY

ANCIENT TIMES

I n Ancient Greece, brides were escorted to their marriage by a group of happily married older women who had already proved their fertility. Young children walked in front of the bride, strewing the ground with grains and herbs to ensure her fertility.

In Ancient Rome; girls walked in front of the bride carrying sheaths of wheat and herbs to ensure fertility and prosperity. At least ten adults, serving as both honor guard and witnesses, accompanied the bride.

How to adapt this for your modern processional

- Have your flower girl(s) carry a posy that includes both wheat and herbs associated with weddings, such as rosemary
- Add wheat and herbs the rose petals your flower girl scatters. This could deliver a bonus. It is easier to get small children to understand the concept of scattering a handful of grain or very small leaves than it is to achieve the same result with rose petals. Children tend to want to pick the petals up one at a time.
- Give all the members of your bridal party rose petals to scatter to ensure a rich carpet of petals. For a lovely visual effect have your flower girl(s) scatter dark petals, your bridesmaids scatter lighter petals, and your MOH scatter

very pale or white petals. The layering of the colors will create a rich and fragrant carpet for you to walk on.

- Consider including older members of your family as attendants, in addition to siblings and younger friends.

In both Greek and Roman weddings, the bride was showered with fruit and nuts, and during a Roman bride's procession to the groom's home, nuts were thrown.

How to adapt this for your modern processional

- Provide your guests with rose petals or bubbles and ask them to shower you as you walk down the aisle.

THE MIDDLE AGES

Throughout Western Europe, it was common that the brides attendants were children. This custom continues to this day in both royal and society weddings.

How to adapt this for your modern processional

- Don't stop at one flower girl. Including several in your bridal party is guaranteed to increase the aaah factor.

Men carrying pennants or banners bearing the family crests of the couple preceded medieval bridal processionals.

How to adapt this for your modern processional

- Have your florist create attach florist foam topiary balls to ¾ inch (20 mm) wooden dowels wrapped with ribbon. Cover the balls with small flowers such as statice, spray roses, button chrysanthemums, ivy, and herbs, and attach floating ribbons. Have your page boys lead the processional, carrying these topiary balls aloft like banners
- Have some or all of your attendants carry helium balloons
- Instead of baskets of petals or posies of flowers, consider letting your flower girls carry pin wheels, ribbon wands, or scaled down topiary balls on sticks.

- Create wedding banner out of cloth. Hang it from a dowel, so that it can be carried at the front of your processional by two flower girls or page boys.

Musicians led the processional or followed the pennant bearers. They played a variety of instruments, including drums, stringed instruments and .wind instruments

How to adapt this for your modern processional

- Hire one or more musicians to lead your processional while playing the music for it.. They can then move to seats set up for them so they can play for the signing of your marriage register (where that is part of the ceremony) and for your recessional.
- Have children walk down the aisle announcing the arrival of the bridal party by ringing bells.

Medieval weddings took place at the church door rather than inside the church, in order to ensure that the ceremony was witnessed. Immediately after the conclusion of the ceremony, the bridal party, chanting a psalm, moved into the church for the celebration of a mass.

How to adapt this for your modern processional

- Choose one of the *songs of ascent* psalms for your processional. In medieval times the choice was usually psalm 128 (127)[7]. When Kate Middleton married Prince William she walked down the aisle to the soaring choral masterpiece "I was glad" by Sir Charles Hubert Hastings Parry from Psalm 122, originally composed for the

---

[7] Protestant churches follow the Hebrew numbering and Catholic and Orthodox churches that of the Greek Septuagint, resulting in minor differences in the numbers. The Greek Septuagint number is given in brackets.

coronation of King Edward VII, and would be a wonderful choice if you have a choir available.

In later Medieval times the ceremony moved inside the church. Before it started, the groom would stand at the church door and, in front of witnesses, commit to the amount of his bride's dower, the portion of his wealth that she would be entitled to should he die before she did.

How to adapt this for your modern processional

- Include a presentation of a gift or token from the groom in the processional. It can be presented on his behalf as you take your first step inside the door. Alternatively he can present it to you when you arrive at the altar.
- Traditionally the groom pays for the bouquets. Have him carry your bouquet with him and present it to you when you arrive at the altar.

On the morning of the wedding, the bridesmaids presented the groom with a bouquet of rosemary (symbolic of love and loyalty.

How to adapt this for your modern processional

- Have each of your bridesmaids carry a small sprig of rosemary and, when they reach the altar, present it to the groom before taking their place.

THE ELIZABETHAN PERIOD

I n Elizabethan times merry minstrels and musicians led the processional. A young girl would walk immediately behind the musicians. She carried a silver bride's cup decorated with ribbons and a branch of gilded rosemary.

How to adapt this for your modern processional

- A pair of flower girls could walk down the aisle together handing out the packets or bags of flowers for your shower of flowers to the guests on either side of the aisle.
- Have your bridesmaids and/or groomsmen carry the items that you will use in a ritual during the ceremony. These could be the cup and the wine for a wine ceremony, the ribbons for handfasting, or the broom, or any other object.

The bridesmaids would make small posies of flowers before the wedding and these or sprigs of rosemary gilded and/or tied with ribbons were handed out to guests as favors.

How to adapt this for your modern processional

- Where the church or wedding venue prohibits scattering or throwing of petals, your flower girls could walk down the aisle handing flowers, sprigs of dried rosemary with the tips spray-painted gold, or little bundles of wedding herbs to guests on both sides of the aisle. A combination of rosemary, basil, marjoram, and sage, tied with a narrow ribbon with a small tag attached explaining the significance of the herbs is a lovely choice.

- The flower girls can carry small bouquets which will be given to the mother of the bride and the mother of the groom.

THE VICTORIAN ERA

The Victorian era was characterized by rigid adherence to etiquette. Those who did not comply with social expectations risked being ostracized. Today, many of those things that are regarded to be 'traditional' for weddings largely stem from this period, though it was usual during that era to be married at home in the parlor, or, if marrying in church, for bride and groom to walk down the aisle together.

The Victorian era was also a time that saw commoditization of all things wedding, along with much else in daily life as the growing middle class sought to impress their peers. This set weddings along the track of becoming the consumer rite of passage accepted as the norm today.

The Nineteenth Century American etiquette book: *Our Deportment: or the Manners Conduct and Dress of the Most Refined Society* by John H. Young, published in 1882, provides a fascinating insight into social expectations about how weddings should be conducted.

The latest New York form for conducting the marriage ceremony is substantially as follows: When the bridal party has arranged itself for entrance, the ushers, in pairs, march slowly up to the altar and turn to the right. Behind them follows the groom alone. When he reaches the altar he turns, faces the aisle, and watches intently for the coming of his bride. After a slight interval the bridesmaids follow, in pairs, and at the altar turn to the left. After another brief interval, the bride, alone and entirely veiled, with her eyes cast down, follows her companions. The groom comes forward a few steps to meet her, takes her hand, and places her at the altar. The parents of the bride, having followed her, stand just behind her and partly to the left.

How to adapt this for your modern processional

- Apart from the suggestion that you walk with your eyes downcast, this form of processional would work well for a modern ceremony.

Young continues: *The ceremonials for the entry to the church by the bridal party may be varied to suit the taste. Precedents for the style already described are found among the highest social circles in New York and other large cities, but there are brides who prefer the fashion of their grandmothers, which is almost strictly an American fashion. In this style, the bridesmaids, each leaning upon the arm of a groomsman, first pass up the aisle to the altar, the ladies going to their left, and the gentlemen to their right. The groom follows with the bride's mother, or someone to represent her, leaning on his arm, whom he seats in a front pew at the left. The bride follows, clinging to the arm of her father (or near relative), or leads her to the groom. The father waits at her left, and a step or two back of her, until asked to give her away, which he does by taking her right hand and placing it in that of the clergyman. After this he joins the mother of the bride in the front pew.*

How to adapt this for your modern processional

- This form of processional works well if you are scheduling 'first look' photographs before the ceremony. It also ensures that your first look moment will be private and more intimate.

Children were a symbolic part of the Victorian wedding. Little girls could be flower girls or ring bearers. If older, they could be junior bridesmaids. They had their own dress etiquette. To symbolize innocence they were always dressed in white, with a ribbon sash that matched their shoes and stockings. Boys, dressed as court pages, had the important role of holding the bride's train. They wore in black, blue, green, or red velvet jackets, knee breech, white silk hose and back shoes with buckles.

How to adapt this for your modern processional

- Include one or two page boys in your processional to walk behind you and manage your train.

PART FIVE:
INVOLVING YOUR GUESTS

WHY INVOLVE YOUR GUESTS?

Guests are an important part of your wedding day. Although it is your day, in a very real sense it also belongs to everyone who loves you. No marriage survives and thrives in isolation. Your guests are at your wedding because they care, because they are important to you and you are important to them. Naturally they want to be part of your wedding, to show their support on this special day and in the years to come. You can facilitate this by making the ceremony inclusive and participatory, by involving your guests as participants rather than an audience for a show.

The growing trend in upselling weddings is all about entertainment at the reception. This conveys the idea that your wedding is a performance designed for maximum entertainment of your guests (as an audience).

Encouraging your guests to participate in your processional will allow them to communicate their happiness for you and to shower you with blessings as you walk down the aisle. This sets a different tone for the whole wedding, not just the ceremony. It will also ensure that you will feel supported and surrounded by love and good will. Your nerves will disappear, your joy will bubble to the surface. You will relax. That can only be a good thing.

SOUND BLESSINGS

In Celtic tradition church bells were rung before the ceremony to ward off evil spirits. It was also believed that bells granted wishes. A rather sweet way to involve your guests is to give each a small bell to "call in the bride and shower her with blessings" or to ring along with the official bell ringer if you are going to announce the processional by having one or more bell ringers walk down the aisle

Ask you your celebrant (officiant) to cue the guests to start ringing their bells just before the processional starts and to continue until the entire bridal party is in place at the altar. The tinkle of small bells will not drown out your processional music but will add to the excitement.

The bells can do double duty if guests are also asked to ring them as you seal your vows with a kiss.

BUBBLE BLESSINGS

I t is relatively common to have your guests shower you with bubbles as the two of you walk back down the aisle after the ceremony. Do something different. Make your entrance through a cloud of bubbles to add a touch of magic to your processional and convey a sense of your intention being blessed by everyone present. This makes for wonderful photographs as you walk towards your groom. For same-sex couples bubbles have an additional symbolism because they incorporate all the colors of the rainbow, albeit subtly.

The blowing of bubbles is permitted by most churches and venues, though it is best to check as some have imposed a ban because of the possibility that carpet and fabric may be stained.

A shower of bubbles works best if the bottles of bubble mixture are neither overly small nor sparsely distributed. Many of the small bottles of bubbles made specifically for weddings come with extremely small openings in the wand. This restricts the size of the bubbles, make it difficult to achieve a shower of bubbles, and requires a level of manual dexterity and hand-eye coordination that may be beyond children and older guests with arthritic hands. Where possible choose bubble bottles that include a flexible wand that opens wide once it is removed from the bottle, allowing larger bubbles to be formed. You might also consider use of a bubble machine discreetly placed about a third of the way down the aisle and pointed back towards the entrance.

Plan ahead to ensure an appropriate density of the bubbles. Place the bubble containers in a prominent position to make sure that your guests will see them as they enter the church or ceremony space. Attach a large sign asking guests to take one and indicating when the bubble shower should occur. For example, *Please take one and shower the bride with bubbles and loving thoughts as she walks down the aisle.* Ask your ushers to reinforce the message by talking guests through what has been planned while handing out the bottles of bubbles. Reinforce the message by adding a small tag to each container, for example *Blessing Bubbles for the entrance of the bride.* You could also include explicit instructions in your Program (Order of Service booklet).

In addition, ask your celebrant (officiant) to coordinate the bubbles. He or she can do this by giving the guests instructions before the ceremony starts.

A Word of Caution:

If the detergent concentration is too high, bubbles can stain delicate fabrics. Minimize the risk of staining by

- Testing the solution to check whether the solution will stain by blowing some bubbles directly at a sample of the fabric. If you do not have a sample of the fabric choose a section of the inside of the hem in an unobtrusive area.
- Purchasing good quality bubble solution from a reputable supplier
- Ensuring that your guests blow the bubbles upwards and above you, rather than directly at you.

SHOWERS OF FLOWERS

S howering newly married couples with the fruits of the earth (grains or flowers) is a very old custom that dates at least as far back as Ancient Egypt, Ancient Greece, Ancient Rome, and parts of the Middle East in ancient times.

During the recessional (the walk out) it is common for guests to shower the bride and groom with rose petals. Throwing of rose petals is also often to enhance the group photograph.

In earlier times, however, it was the bride who was showered with flowers or grain. Flowers and herbs were strewn in her path as she walked to her wedding. This custom still survives in the rose-petal strewn aisle, or when flower girls scatter rose petals on the floor, the carpet, or the grass for the bride to walk on as she makes her way down the aisle.

There is no ceremonial reason why you can't involve the guests in showering the bride with flowers as she enters the church, chapel, or ceremony space, however, it would be wise to consult with your venue before making any decisions. Some venues ban all tosses because of clean-up problems and the risks associated with petals, seeds, and grains, and may charge a hefty clean-up fee if the ban is ignored. Others may allow only biodegradable tosses, but some may ban fresh petals due to potential staining of carpets or risk of guests slipping and falling, but allow dried or silk petals.

Rose petals

Roses are symbolic of love. Scattering rose petals is a visual representation of the blessing of family and friends. A shower of rose petals raises the romantic temperature of your processional and adds a touch of luxury.

Fresh, Freeze-dried, or Silk?

For a rose-petal toss you have the choice of using fresh rose petals, freeze-dried rose petals or artificial rose petals (silk or polyester). Your budget, whether you will be using the petals indoors or outdoors, the policy of the venue, whether you are going to have the petals put in place before you walk down the aisle, scattered in your path as you walk down the aisle, or showered over you, together with personal preference, will drive your decision as to which type of petals will be best.

For outdoor ceremonies, both fresh or freeze-dried petals are appropriate because they are natural and biodegradable. For indoor ceremonies freeze dried or silk rose petals are more appropriate because they are easier to clean up, do not stain as long as they remain dry, and are less slippery than fresh petals.

Fresh Rose Petals:

- Are most expensive of the three types if purchase as petals because you will be paying for the labor of removing the petals from the roses just before use. To save money, buy roses and delegate the de-petaling to friends or family members who are able to complete this task on your wedding day.
- Have a rich softness missing from the other types.
- Are biodegradable.
- Will lose their freshness fast, particularly in hot or humid weather or if the roses were on their last legs

before being de-petaled, so they must be obtained on the day of use, and even then there is a possibility that they may not look good by the time they are used.

- Can be difficult or impossible to obtain at some times of the year, or in mid-winter, or around Valentine's Day, when they will also be much more expensive,
- Can stain fabrics, carpets and flooring.
- Can be slippery.

Freeze-dried Rose Petals

- Are the mid-price petals, not as expensive as fresh but more expensive than silk.
- Are a long lasting alternative to fresh with the look and feel of fresh petals. They will fade over time, especially if exposed to light and humidity, so avoid have them delivered too far ahead, and refrain from opening them until the day before the ceremony.
- Are a healthy option as any bacterial or fungal infestation is eliminated by the drying process.
- Can be ordered and received several weeks before the wedding.
- Are lighter than fresh or artificial petals and therefore take longer to float through the air, thus increasing the chance of great photographs of both scattering and showering.
- Are less likely to stain or cause gets to slip and fall, however, if it is raining, they will rehydrate. This will increase the possibility that they will cause stains and that they will become slippery.

Artificial Rose Petals

- Generally, the least expensive of the three options, but you get what you pay for with silk rose petals. Cheap silk petals can look cheap, feel thin, will all be the same size, or even be almost transparent. Better quality silk rose petals will vary in size and won't be transparent. Look for petals made of a microfiber peach silk, giving them the texture and the weight of real rose petals.

- Will never decay, so you can obtain them well ahead of your wedding date.

A word of caution:

Some suppliers suggest that you can soften freeze-dried petals before using them by opening the night before the wedding and exposing them to the air, or by placing them in the bathroom while taking a shower. These tactics will make the petals softer and more pliable (but not as soft as fresh petals). The longer they are exposed to humidity the softer they will become and the brighter darker colored petals will become. But be aware, softening petals this way can make them more slippery and more likely to stain, and will make them heavier, so that they will be less effective because they will descend more quickly than drier petals.

Other flowers

While rose petals are the more usual choice, they are by no means the only choice for your shower of flowers. If you are marrying in winter, or close to Valentine's Day, when prices rise and supply may be made more difficult by the high demand for roses, you may wish to consider alternatives, either on their own, or mixed with rose petals.

Companies that market freeze-dried petals continue to expand the range of petals available. Many now offer delphinium and larkspur blossoms, allowing you to add an all-natural *something blue* touch. The advantage of using freeze-dried petals is two-fold. Because the process removes moisture, the petals are much lighter than fresh petals and therefore they float through the air more slowly. Freeze-drying also extends the season when the petals are available.

Some of the more common alternatives to rose petals include bougainvillea, hydrangea, and lavender. Jasmine blossoms and miniature button chrysanthemums are growing in popularity. You can also create your own unique petal mix.

Bougainvillea

Bougainvillea "petals" (to be accurate, bracts), are lighter than rose petals. When thrown they linger in the air longer than any other type of petal, ensuring that even the slowest photographer will get a picture. They come in a wide range of bright and pastel colors, including white, and are available for many months of the year. In warmer climates you could probably source them at no cost from the gardens of family and friends.

Carnations

Carnations, which in the Victorian language of flowers symbolize pure love, are very easy to use. Their ragged petals create a nice textural contrast to smooth rose petals when used in a mixed petal toss. At one time carnations were believed to be an aphrodisiac and therefore they are linked with fertility. Their spicy clove fragrance makes them particularly nice to walk on as crushing them releases the fragrance.

Hydrangeas

Hydrangeas are available freeze-dried in a range of colors, including green. Though there are differences of opinion as to the symbolic meaning of this flower, the one that is most appropriate to weddings is that it represents any wish that is sincerely heartfelt.

Lavender

.Lavender and rose petals have long been regarded to be a natural pairing. According to ancient literature, Cleopatra, Queen of Egypt, used a fragrance incorporating both rose and lavender to seduce both Julius Caesar and Mark Anthony. .In the language of flowers lavender represents love, loyalty, and devotion. Lavender as a color symbolizes spirituality, creativity, mindfulness, perception and spiritual connection with others, so showering a bride with lavender buds adds more than fragrance and color.

Jasmine
Of all the flowers used for flower showers, jasmine has the strongest fragrance, reflecting its symbolic meaning of sensuality, grace, and elegance. Use the flowers whole.

Button Chrysanthemums
The flower symbolism of chrysanthemums is abundance, hope, and wonderful friendship. The Japanese put a single chrysanthemum petal in the bottom of a wine glass to sustain a long and healthy life.

Mixed Flower Showers
You can use a mixture of petals to add variety, or when it is not possible to obtain enough of a particular petal to meet your needs. Choose four to six different flowers and herbs to create a toss that symbolizes the specific blessings you hope for your marriage. While many herbs have leaves of similar sizes to flower petals, where the leaves are tiny, such as in thyme, rather than stripping the tiny leaves off the stems, clip tiny sprigs of similar size to the petals in your mix to ensure that the mix doesn't separate in the cone or bag.

Any two types of petals can be mixed in equal quantities by volume. Good combinations are rose petals and lavender, rose petals and jasmine, or bougainvillea and hydrangeas.

For balance in a mixture use equal quantities by volume of four different petals and/or herbs and then add an equal amount of rose petals (for example one cup each of carnation petals, lavender, jasmine flowers and sage leaves and 4 cups of rose petals.

Strewing herbs
Herbs have been associated with weddings, and specifically with good wishes and blessings for thousands of years. In ancient times,

herbs were used in garlands and wreaths. In the Middle Ages, the entire path from the bride's home to the church was carpeted in soft rushes, herbs and flower petals. In the Victorian era, a mix of herbs and petals were thrown as the couple left the church.

Today, as couples increasingly look for in-expensive and earth-friendly traditions to incorporate in their weddings, herbs are making a comeback as a romantic and aromatic alternative to more expensive flowers. Using herbs adds the color green, associated with nature, fertility, abundance, good fortune, generosity, and prosperity, and the symbolic color of wealth.

Using herbs rather than flowers can also ensure that you avoid the residues of pesticides that may remain on flowers, pesticides that can cause reactions in some guests. At certain times of the year most herbs flower, producing small white or pink blossoms.

You can purchase fresh herbs at supermarkets, produce stores, or farmers markets. Dried herbs also work well, as long as the leaves are dried whole. You can dry the herbs yourself if you have a cool, dry, place where you can suspend the bunches head down and allow them to dry naturally.

You might find one of the following ways to dry herbs is more appropriate to your situation:

- Fill a box with sand (clean white sand available from a pet store is a good choice). Place the herbs on the sand and sift more sand over until the herbs are completely covered.
- Place the herbs in the oven at a very low temperature until dry. The temperature should be the lowest temperature your oven can achieve because you do not want to cook the herbs. You will need to experiment.
- Place the herbs in an airtight container and cover with silica gel crystals for an extended period.
- Use a home-food-drying appliances.

Avoid the bottles of dried herbs for sale in the spice aisle of your supermarket. Those herbs tend to be either ground or shredded into small particles that are far too fine for use to either scatter in the aisle or shower over a bride.

Good wedding herbs include:

Basil

This popular culinary herb symbolizes love and good wishes. The word *basil* derives from the Greek and means *king*.

Marjoram

Legend has it that Aphrodite, the Greek goddess of love, created marjoram as a symbol of happiness. As a result, the Greeks crowned young couples with wreaths of marjoram, leading to an association with weddings.

Rosemary

While rosemary has become associated primarily with remembrance, in ancient times this herb also represented love and fidelity and consequently it has been used in weddings throughout the ages. In Mexico, rosemary is grown as a good-luck charm.

Sage

Sage has long symbolized long life, good health, and domestic virtue.

How to ensure a successful shower of flowers

Ensuring a successful shower of flowers requires consultation with your venue, a choice of flowers that is appropriate to the venue, a decision as to whether the flowers will be scattered in your path or showered over you, careful preparation and coordination on the day.. Taking care of these aspects will ensure a successful shower of flowers that is captured for posterity in photographs that convey the emotion of the moment.

Weight counts

The lighter the individual petal, the better it will float and the longer it will remain airborne. Heavier items fall faster, lighter more slowly. The longer petals remain in the air, the better chance your photographer and your guests with cameras will have of capturing great images.

Visualize the moment

Visualize the shower of flowers. Do you want one or more flower girls to scatter the flowers in your path? Do you want your guests to toss the flowers in your path as you approach them, or up into the air so that the petals float down on you like a blessing as you move down the aisle?

Rehearse the flower girls

Do not rely only on verbal instructions. Children often pick up one petal at a time and drop each very carefully if not thoroughly rehearsed in grabbing the petals by the handful and scattering them as if they are feeding chickens.

Present the flowers effectively

Flower tosses are most commonly presented in individual petal cones that are put out for guests to take as they enter the ceremony venue, handed to guests, or placed on their seats. Cones are a popular choice because they are easy to use, requiring use of one hand only and a simple underhand tossing motion. Bags and envelopes require guests to pour the petals into their hands before throwing or scattering them.

While many different styles of petal cones are available commercially, and it is possible to buy petal cones already filled with fresh or freeze-dried, it does not require a great deal of skill to make your own. They are just a piece of paper rolled into a cone. To do this all you need to know is that you start at one side of the sheet of paper and roll it towards the side of the sheet that is at a 90° angle, that is, roll the right corner in towards the left corner. The pointed end of the cone lies at the corner where the two sides meet. If you prefer a flat end rather than a point, simply fold over the pointed end and tape or glue it into place.

Choose thicker paper so that your cones has some body. Translucent vellum, flocked, embossed, or flower pressed paper add a classy touch to petal cones. Pages of old books or sheets of music can speak to your personal interests or the theme of your wedding.

You can also use cellophane bags, glassine envelopes, organza favor bags, muslin or calico bags.

Cellophane and glassine bags are cheap and sturdy, and because they're transparent, show off the toss to good effect, and allow you to print instructions on a piece of paper almost as big as the bag. Cut the paper just slightly narrower than the bag in order to ensure a snug fit, and short enough to allow the top inch and a half to be gathered and tied with a ribbon, or folded over and secured with a sticker.

Drawstring bags work well for lavender buds, however, they do not work particularly well for rose petals unless the opening is large enough to allow a guest to take a handful of petals out of the bag. Bags can prove a challenge to female guests who may be juggling a purse and a wrap as well as the toss, because they require two free hands., so do not double-knot the drawstrings. Just pull the drawstrings tight so guests can get to the toss quickly and easily.

Boxes work relatively well for all tosses. Because the top is open guests can easily transfer the toss from the box to their hands, or they can toss direct from an open box using an underhand toss.

Provide Instructions

The success of your shower of flowers depends largely on the technique used to throw or deliver the petals. A good rule of thumb is that petals and herbs should be tossed above you (and slightly ahead of you so they float down onto you where you are, not where you've just been. An underhand toss, aiming the petals high above the heads of head of the bride, works well. An overhand throw angles the petals on a downward trajectory, straight for the bride's face, so should be avoided. To scatter petals on the aisle ahead of the bride, guests should be encouraged to use the same technique as the flower girls, using a sideways hand movement as if scattering grain to feed chickens.

Add a tag or label to your petal cones, bags, envelopes, or sachets to alert guests as to when and how you would like them to use the contents.

Nominate leaders

Ask selected close friends to lead the way. Brief them thoroughly so that they can position themselves in the right place to give the rest of the guests the cue to follow their example.

Ensure everyone has what is needed and when it is needed

Place the bubble bottles or petals where guests will be sure to see them. Add a sign so that guests know they are expected to pick one up. Alternatively have someone hand them to guests, or place them on seats.

Ask adults to supervise children

Children may get carried away with the excitement and start throwing the petals too early. Encourage adults to keep custody of the petals or bubbles until the last moment.

PRACTICAL CONSIDERATIONS

Y ou will need to calculate how many containers of flowers you will need, and what volume of petals will be required to fill them. You will also need to identify appropriate sources, arrange for delivery or collection, and delegate helpers to package the tosses ready for the ceremony.

To ensure your shower is as fresh and lovely as possible keep both flowers and fresh herbs in water. Cut the stems diagonally and plunge into cool water immediately after they delivered. Strip the petals as close to the wedding time as possible, definitely no earlier than the morning of the wedding.

If using dried petals ignore any instructions to open and expose to the air to allow the petals to soften. Instead, keep the package sealed until the last possible moment so the petals will remain as dry and light as possible and will therefore take longer to drift to the ground after being tossed.

Fill cones or bags the day of the wedding, preferably as close to the time of the wedding as is practical. This is a task you can and should delegate.

Calculating what you need

If presenting the flowers already packaged in a cone or bag, for petal and herb showers you will need about ½ cup of fresh or freeze-dried flower petals per cone/bag. For silk rose petals allow 12 per guest.

How to remove petals from flowers

As you remove the petals drop them in a broad flat container, such as a basket, to ensure that the petals are not crushed or bruised.

Roses

Ensure that the roses are slightly soft. With one hand, hold the rose stem up close to the base of the rose. With your other hand cup the rose head and carefully pull the head to one side. You will find that all the petals will come off together with minimal damage, leaving the core of the rose (the stamens) attached to the stem.

Carnations and daisies

Gently grasp the flower stem near the head. Grasp several petals between the thumb and fingers of the other hand and carefully pull out the petals.

APPENDIX

WORKSHEET: Our Processional participants

Participants and order of our processional

Who will notify the celebrant (officiant) that the bride has arrived?

How?

Who will cue the start of the music?

How?

Who will cue the processional?

How?

WORKSHEET: Our Processional Music

Who will provide the music?

Live   Recorded

☐ Singer accompanied by   ☐ **CD Player**

_____   ☐ **iPod**

☐ Solo Musician

☐ Type of instrument

_____

☐ Duo

☐ Type of instruments

_____

_____

☐ Trio

☐ Type of instruments

_____

_____

☐ Quartet

☐ Type of instruments

_____

_____

☐ Quintent

☐ Type of instruments

_____

_____

☐ Mixed

     ☐ Type _____

Name and contact details of musician(s) or person responsible for operating the recorded music

Music choice for entrance of the Bridal Party

Music choice for entrance of the bride

Music choice for entrance of the groom

WORKSHEET: Our Processional Shower

Type of Shower

Shower

- ☐ Bubbles
- ☐ Petals
  - ☐ Type _____
- ☐ Herbs
  - ☐ Type _____
- ☐ Mixed
  - ☐ Type _____

Container

- ☐ Box
- ☐ Calico/Muslin Bag
- ☐ Cellophane Bag
- ☐ Cone
- ☐ Glassine Envelope
- ☐ Organza Bag
- ☐ Other

Where and when will the shower take place

Who will participate

Supplies required

Suppliers

ABOUT THE AUTHOR

Jennifer Cram is a professional marriage celebrant (wedding officiant) appointed by the Attorney General to officiate marriages in all states and territories of Australia. She is currently based in Brisbane, Queensland, where each year she creates and officiates more than a hundred marriage ceremonies. She also officiates numerous commitment ceremonies for same sex couples.

Born in Australia and raised in Africa, Jennifer (or Jenny as she is known to her family, her friends, and the couples she works with) comes from a family that for five generations has moved between Australia, Africa and the United States. One of her great-great-grandfathers was a forty-niner, her great-grandfather and her great-uncle worked on the reconstruction of San Francisco after the 1906 earthquake, and she herself lived for some time in New York City as a young woman. A skilled and experienced writer, public speaker, and choreographer, Jennifer has numerous academic qualifications in Celebrancy and holds degrees in Literature, Psychology, Information Science, and Management. She brings all those skills to the development and performance of ceremonies, together her knowledge and experience of multiple cultures and sensitivity to cultural nuances.

Appreciated by wedding photographers for her attention to the visual aspects of the ceremony and for the way she ensures photogenic moments of warm and natural interaction between the couple and between the couple, their bridal party, and the guests, she has devoted a great deal of time to researching and developing a wide range of alternative ways to include and personalize rituals in ceremonies.

To learn more about Jennifer or enquire about booking her for a ceremony go to www.jennifercram.com.au or read on for some comments from photographers and couples:

Got a lot of comments like best wedding EVER and that was from a 60 year old man lol. Loved it and loved you. - **Casie and Nathan**

Jenny I have had the pleasure of working with you many times and I can honestly say that every time has been beautiful, intimate and personal. Experience counts for a lot, but it isn't just experience or the age of a person that makes a ceremony for a couple, it is a person who has a beautiful soul and puts that into their work that truly makes it a unforgettable and personal experience for the couples. The genuine emotions that you bring out in couples are such beautiful moments for them to share and from a photographers standpoint make our job even more special to be able to be part of and document for our couples. - **Scott Lawler of Scott Lawler Photography**

We couldn't have asked for a more personal, thoughtful ceremony. Jennifer managed to include humorous and light hearted moments in the ceremony without losing the sense of occasion or solemnity. We are so grateful to Jenny for making our wedding ceremony such a special and memorable occasion and will be recommending her to all of our friends. - **Rebecca and Tom**

Jennifer Cram is a shining example of excellence in her profession. Her ability to listen, ask the <u>right</u> questions and gently guide us produced the perfect ceremony. Every part of the ceremony was infused with Darren and my personalities. We have received countless comments from guests about our ceremony and their impression of Jenny, all glowing and very touching. I even had one friend say she was 'hanging on Jenny's every word. Jenny Cram helped make such perfect memories for all at our wedding. We are deeply indebted. -**Jannine and Darren**

We were lucky enough to have Jennifer Cram design and conduct our commitment ceremony recently and highly recommend that you secure her services before you even begin to plan your special day! In addition to being a lovely lady and a genuine support of same sex marriage, Jenny is a true professional with the ability to use her experience and talent to ensure that your ceremony is unique and special to you and your partner alone. Our friends and family say that they enjoyed feeling including in the occasion and that it seem like Jenny knew Gabby and I personally. Many of them also said it was one of the most moving and beautiful ceremonies that they had been to because of the insight it gave into our relationship and love for each other. And this is what sets Jenny apart from all of the other celebrants! In addition to all of the above, Jenny gave us the guidance and resources we needed to create the perfect ceremony for us, and was always responsive and accommodating to our needs. We are truly grateful to Jenny for making our ceremony a special one and we know that you will be too! - **Nicole and Gabby**

We asked Jenny for a simple ceremony that was no fuss yet still memorable to us and she delivered. We are so grateful that she took care in what we wanted but still added a little touch of her own magic to make our day one that we would never forget. Thank you for a beautiful day! We enjoyed every moment. Jenny created a ceremony that was unique for us and we didn't feel pressured into doing anything we didn't want to do. it was good that we could have a laugh as well, that was very important to us. - **Terese and Dion**

From our very first phone call to Jennifer we found her approach to be comfortable, calm and competent, whilst being professional yet personal. These thoughts were proved during our first face-to-face meeting. Communication frequency was appropriate. We had given Jennifer specific ideas and expectations of her as a Celebrant and at no time were we disappointed with her suggestions and ideas and final product. Jennifer conducted the ceremony in such manner allowing our love to shine. Barely a dry eye in the house our guests commented it was the best, most meaningful, personalised civil ceremony they have ever attended. We would have absolutely no hesitation in recommending Jennifer. We provide this testimonial with our heartfelt thanks. Kind regards and love - **Craig & James**

In all honesty we were merely looking for a registry marriage alternative when we were searching for a celebrant but boy were we in for a treat when we found Jenny Cram. The idea of getting married in a registry office seemed cold, robotic, and just downright uncomfortable so we opted to find a celebrant to marry us in a more relaxed atmosphere. Having never searched for a celebrant before we found that most treated the matter pretty much the same as the registry office would, the only difference being the backdrop, so we were very excited to find a celebrant who took to treating our prospective marriage with the same level of courtesy, consideration, and compassion as if we were a wealthy couple seeking the best kind of marriage money could buy. We were expecting a quick and regimented procedure but Jenny was very patient and thorough with us making sure we were clear and understanding of every detail and nuance of the process in the most painless and pleasurable manner we could have hoped for. What seemed like a confusing kaleidoscope of legal requirements was a smooth and easy experience under Jenny's comfortable guidance. The day of our wedding was pure magic and on that day it became clear that Jenny was a passionate and seasoned professional dedicated to serving our marriage with the warmest reverence. We never imagined a minimalist wedding could be so special. We are forever grateful to Jenny for effortlessly transforming our marriage from what could have been an economy class experience into an unforgettable day of enchantment. - **Clint and Hyejin**

Jenny was extremely open and understanding of our unconventional circumstances from the beginning. She welcomed us into her home and impressed us with her vast knowledge and experience, not only to our ceremony but also with her knowledge regarding our different cultural heritages and the history of the local area. She also had fantastic ideas of how to incorporate her knowledge into our ceremony to make it unique to us. She remained constantly in touch with us throughout the planning process, always ready to bestow her wisdom, even encouraging us to be more romantic in our vows. On the day she was a calming presence and the way she took control made us feel like the day was in safe hands. Finally, her personal and intimate touch at the end of the ceremony was an incredible surprise, very touching and well beyond the call of duty. She was incredible and I would recommend her to other couples without a second thought. - **Gael and Ryan**

www.ingramcontent.com/pod-product-compliance
Lightning Source LLC
Chambersburg PA
CBHW060150300526
45790CB00014B/482